Slayer of the Soul

Stephen J. Rossetti

Slayer of the Soul

Child Sexual Abuse and the Catholic Church

XXIII
TWENTY-THIRD PUBLICATIONS
Mystic, Connecticut

Twenty-Third Publications
185 Willow Street
P.O. Box 180
Mystic, CT 06355
(203) 536-2611

ISBN 0-89622-452-X
Library of Congress Catalog Card Number 90-70990

Foreword

Sean D. Sammon, F.M.S., Ph.D.

Two very different books about teachers were published recently. In Tracy Kidder's *Among School Children*, we eavesdrop on the classes of Christine Zajac, an elementary teacher at the Kelly School in Holyoke, Massachusetts. This young woman does something wonderful for the boys and girls entrusted to her care: she teaches them to believe in themselves.

Lisa Manshel's *Nap Time* is a book of a very different sort. In this work we read about the systematic sexual abuse of children, ages 3–5, who attended the Wee Care Day Nursery in Maplewood, New Jersey, one of the wealthiest areas of the state. Margaret Kelly Michaels, about whom the book is written, was an inexperienced 23-year-old teacher who was eventually convicted on 131 counts of sexual abuse. She left the children in her care a different legacy: at the very least, she robbed them of their childhood.

Now, in a third book, *Slayer of the Soul: Child Sexual Abuse and the Catholic Church*, we have a most useful volume that illuminates for us the essential background of the recently emerging phenomenon of the sexual abuse of children.

The results of the enactment of child abuse reporting laws indicate widespread sexual exploitation of children and adolescents. A questionnaire distributed during the late 1970s to a group of college students revealed that, prior to their eighteenth birthday, nearly one in five of the women and one in eleven of the men had had a sexual experience with an adult. Surveys conducted during the years since then yield figures that cause many to criticize those early estimates as too conservative.

Television documentaries and expanded press coverage about the sexual abuse of children, as well as a startling increase in reported abuse since 1976, cause the public to wonder whether an epidemic of abuse is sweeping the nation. The ever-increasing number of widely publicized arrests for sexually abusive behavior has also sensitized the general population. Especially shocking has been the arrest of teachers, child care workers, priests and male religious, and others to whom the welfare of children has been entrusted.

Church leaders have special pastoral responsibilities when dealing with sexual abuse, particularly when it involves a colleague. Their obligations extend not only to victims, their families, and the perpetrators of abuse, but to all men and women ministering in the church community who need to continue their work free of suspicion.

To act responsibly, church leaders need to learn the facts about child sexual abuse. As a necessary first step, comprehensive education can provide them with important tools for intervention, treatment, and prevention. *Slayer of the Soul* will help them in that task. Bringing together experts from mental health, law, pastoral theology, and medicine, this book helps answer these five questions:

1. What is child sexual abuse?
2. Who are the victims of this behavior?
3. Who are the perpetrators?
4. What help exists for each group?
5. What is the church's responsibility in the process of healing?

Scope of the Problem

Researchers in the field point out that abuse occurs when dependent, developmentally immature children and adolescents become involved in sexual activity which they do not understand fully and to which they cannot freely give informed consent. This behavior often violates the social taboos of family roles.

Victims of child sexual abuse come from all races, creeds, and socio-economic levels. Victims may be white, black, Hispanic, or Asian, Catholic or Protestant, rich or poor, male or female, (although for every boy, two or three girls are reportedly victimized). Abuse typically begins at age 8 or 9, and lasts about five years. Boys are more commonly victimized by someone outside their families, whereas girls are often abused by someone within the home. Some children are threatened with punishment if they fail to cooperate; others are manipulated and told the activity is a game or something "special" and fun.

Child sexual abuse falls into several categories: incest, exhibitionism, molestation, rape, sexual sadism, and child pornography and prostitution. More than 300,000 children in the United States are involved in child prostitution and pornography alone. Even though reporting laws have increased sensitivity to the victimization of minors, child sexual abuse continues to be vastly underreported.

The adults who abuse children cover a wide spectrum. Psychologist David Finkelhor points out that they include the man who spends his whole life fixated on 8-year-old boys as well as the one who convinces his girlfriend to bring a child into their bed to "experience something new." Children are the sole erotic interest of some adults; others become involved only under extraordinary circumstances.

Patterns of Abuse
Child sexual abuse expert Suzanne Sgroi points out that sexual encounters between adults and children usually follow a predictable pattern: *engagement, sexual interaction, secrecy, disclosure,* and *suppression.* Perpetrators look for opportunities to be alone with children and engage in sexual activity. After victimization, most perpetrators impose secrecy, which eliminates accountability and enables repetition of the behavior. Following the disclosure, perpetrators usually respond with alarm to the secret's revelation, and family members ask, "How will this situation affect me (us)?" Those who are secure and emotionally strong will move toward the victim with concern and protection. Others, already aware of the abuse or perhaps participants in it, react with guilt or out of self-interest. Families need enormous support to maintain a victim-oriented response.

A suppression phase often follows the disclosure. Whether the abuse happened within or outside the family, members may try to suppress publicity, information, and intervention. Some deny the significance of the abuse suffered by the child and discourage further intervention by outsiders who wish to help.

About 85 percent of all perpetrators are male, from every profession and trade. Many are described as "me-first" individuals who find sexual relationships with children safer and less threatening than relationships with peers.

When is the best time for a person sexually attracted to children to seek help? *Today.* Even for those who have never acted on the impulses they have, professional assistance is available. With it, they can be helped before any child is victimized.

The Church's Role

Speaking at a seminar entitled "Suffer the Children: Sexual Misconduct of Ministers in the Catholic Community," Attorney F. Ray Mouton, made this comment:

> We must remember at all times that children are entrusted to us, all of us, by God, and when a perpetrator sexually molests a child, be that person a lay person, a cleric or religious, the very first thing that is taken from that child is God's greatest gift, innocence.

Whenever child sexual abuse occurs, *church ministers need to assist abuse victims and their families, as well as the abusers.* Serving as administrators, pastors, teachers, health care workers, and counselors, they are ideally situated to observe possible abuse situations and to arrange for intervention and treatment of both victim and victimizer. Swift and responsible action in any current abuse situation can prevent tragedy for others later.

Dioceses and religious communities need to develop procedures for evaluation and intervention to handle reports of child sexual abuse. In this, professional clinical and legal advice should be sought. When the abuser is a priest or religious, prompt and informed action is necessary. Religious leaders have the responsibility to investigate any suspicion of abuse, to adhere to the letter and spirit of state reporting laws, and to make available to all involved adequate evaluation and treatment.

The person who becomes sexually involved with children is scorned, stigmatized, and condemned. Few people apparently wish to discover the behavior's cause, let alone show compassion, forgiveness, and provide help. *Slayer of the Soul* takes steps to counter that apathy. It points out well that the church community can provide leadership in this area, recalling the message of Jesus that, instead of apathy or even revenge, decisive action, compassion, healing, and reformation are called for.

Acknowledgments

Heartfelt thanks to the many people who helped this work come to fruition, especially Joe Champlin, Jeanne Corrigan, John Nash, Will Pilette, Helene Rossetti, Linda Schmidt, and Arlene Vannie. I extend my gratitude to my Ordinary, Bishop O'Keefe, for his continued support and guidance. And a note of thanks to the committed people of Twenty-Third Publications who believed in this project from the beginning and who supported it at every phase.

Contents

This poem was written by a child molester.

Slayer of the Soul

I am the slayer of the soul
destroyer of the dream
The nightmares which recur
and wake you with your screams.

I am the end of innocence
the planting of the fear
That eats away inside your mind
and kills you year by year.

I am the words you cannot speak
the acts that you regret
The twisted childhood memories
that you cannot forget.

I am the terror in your voice
as painfully you plea
To fight the urges inside of you
to end up just like me.

(See p. 19, "Psychological Theories of Pedophilia and Ephebophil-ia" by L.M. Lothstein, Ph.D.)

Slayer of the Soul

Introduction

Stephen J. Rossetti, D.Min.

From reading the newspapers and watching television talk shows, it may appear that the priesthood and religious life have an alarmingly high number of child molesters. The names of priests who are child molesters are revealed to the public; each incident is followed with vigor, and such cases invariably make national news. Recently, an appalling situation was publicized in which a group of religious were accused of belonging to a ring of child molesters. Everywhere we turn, it appears that priests and religious are being accused, sometimes convicted, and imprisoned on charges of child sexual abuse.

For a clergy that is already suffering from a crisis of morale and declining vocations, this is deemed to be a death knell. For a society that has difficulty trusting in authority figures, including religious ones, this is one more reason to stop listening to and trusting their voices. For a church that is struggling to adapt to the changes in society, it is a crisis that no one expected or quite knows how to handle.

As strange as it might seem, we should be grateful to the television talk shows, the media in general, and to our legal system; they have done us a service. They have forced us to face an issue that has too long been buried. The church, like the greater society, has not understood the illness that brings about child molestation and the searing damage that it causes. The media have brought this illness into the open; our legal system has made the penalty for ignoring it too high; and the ensuing public outcry gives testimony to the urgency of this issue. There *is* a problem of child sexual abuse in our church, and we cannot ignore it.

A Devastating and Powerful Disease

An older pastor told me that, a few years ago, a young priest assigned to his parish had been caught sexually abusing children. The pastor said that, at the time, no one quite knew what to do about it. The young priest, however, subsequently announced that he himself had taken care of the situation. He had gone to confession and the problem was over. The pastor felt uncomfortable with this solution but did not know what further steps to take. Not surprisingly, the young priest was caught in the act again. Although confession cleanses the soul, it does not always heal mental illness.

The church is at the same place with sexual abuse problems that it was a few decades ago with the problem of alcohol. If a priest had a "drinking problem" thirty years ago, the bishop disciplined him. The priest was admonished to exercise more "self-control." Excessive drinking was considered a fault of character or simply a lack of effort. We slowly came to realize, however, that alcoholism is a devastating and powerful disease that cannot be cured, but only controlled. The alcoholic needs a supportive yet challenging environment, a rigorous treatment program, and the wisdom of Alcoholics Anonymous to cope with this disease.

We are only beginning to understand the illness that brings about the sexual abuse of children. But our initial findings point to a process not unlike an addiction to alcohol. It stems from an inner psychic and/or biological dysfunction. It winds its way through an individual's system much like poison through a living organism. It causes the individual to be blind to the disease, to be unaware of the self-destructive behavior it causes, and to be unable to acknowledge the devastation inflicted on others. Finally, the illness ends in the perpetrator's own psychic death unless active and vigorous steps are taken to stop the advancement of the disease.

It is difficult to confront someone with an illness of which he or she is not consciously aware. Anyone who has confronted alcoholics with the truth of their disease knows that the likely responses include ardent denials, complex rationalizations, and intense hostility. Confronting the child molester is not much different. Its extreme legal and social consequences make it even more distasteful, and persons more resistant to treatment. Child sexual abuse is an issue with which we prefer not to become involved.

A priest mentioned to me that he had been in the unfortunate circumstance of having to report an incidence of child sexual abuse. A teenage girl revealed to him that her father had been sexually "touching" her. Reluctantly, the priest reported the case and the father was eventually jailed. With the father gone, the family was broken apart and the remaining members had a difficult time supporting themselves financially. The priest was not sure he had done the right thing and he felt very guilty.

During the course of the investigation, however, much more damaging evidence was uncovered. It turned out that the father had not just molested his one daughter by "touching" her. He had sexual intercourse with her repeatedly and was doing so until he was arrested. It also was revealed that he was abusing his younger daughters as well. It was only the priest's report that stopped the abuse.

When child sexual abuse is first uncovered, the initial facts usually represent the "tip of the iceberg," as this priest found out. In a pivotal study (Abel *et al.*, 1987), people suffering from sexual deviant behaviors were asked to reveal the sexual crimes they had committed. Confidentiality was assured and they were granted immunity from prosecution. When these people revealed the extent of their hidden crimes, researchers were stunned.

This study revealed 377 child molesters who committed sexual acts against children *outside their homes.* These 377 adults had victimized a total of 4,435 girls and 22,981 boys. They were guilty of 5,197 acts of abuse against the girls and 43,100 against the boys. The study also included 203 perpetrators who were sexually involved with children *within the home* (incest). These 203 incest perpetrators accosted 286 female victims and 75 male victims. They committed a total of 12,927 incestuous acts against the girls and 2,741 against the boys. As such research shows, child sexual abuse is rarely an isolated event.

Two years later, Fuller's work (1989) confirmed these findings. He stated, "A single child molester may commit hundreds of sexual acts on hundreds of children." *To report one abuser is perhaps to save scores of future victims.* It is imperative that we face squarely the issue of child molestation and report any incidents through the proper channels. They most often represent not isolated incidents but a pervasive pattern of abuse.

Although we can thank the media for helping to make us aware of this important issue, we realize that the media are not equipped to present the complexities of this phenomenon nor provide a balanced perspective from which to view it. The makeup of our society and the limitations of television and daily newspapers lead to an emphasis on the most sensational news. Complex events are treated with few nuances and many generalizations, giving impressions that are not always accurate.

Even though the vast majority of the cases of child sexual abuse occur in the home, the ones that make the news are the ones that grab public attention. A priest of the Roman Catholic church who molests a child is headline news. A father molesting his teenage daughter is not. There are well over 50,000 priests and religious brothers in the United States. As of March 1990, only 73 cases of child molestation against a priest or religious in the United States have entered the legal system. While others have been settled out of court, it is clear that the percentage of church ministers involved in child molestation is very low. A young boy or girl is much more likely to be sexually abused by the father of the family than by the parish priest.

The notoriety that accompanies such church cases does not seem fair. Perhaps it is not. But this notoriety must be expected because priests and religious are public figures. They occupy a special position of public trust with rights and privileges attached to it. Likewise, they must bear the responsibilities that accompany these privileges. They need to know that they are subject to public scrutiny and public notoriety for their actions.

A Higher Moral Standard

In addition, the public expects a higher standard of morality from its public figures, especially its ministers of religion. In a recent trial of a priest accused of child sexual abuse, the prosecutor argued for a prison term because, "as a priest...[he] was in a position of trust." While the judge gave a suspended sentence partly based on the defendant's decision to undergo psychological treatment, he agreed that "people expect better conduct from 'a person in holy orders'" (*Kitchener-Waterloo Record*, 1989).

If this expectation of a higher standard of conduct is found within our society, it is likely that priests and religious expect a higher standard of conduct from themselves as well. This has, indeed, been my observation. What we forgive in others, we do not forgive in ourselves. And the press is painfully reminding us that we are not able to live up to this higher standard. The accompanying shame and self-denigration felt by many church ministers can be severe and can have a serious impact on church morale.

In the pre-Vatican II days, it was common to believe that the priest was a cut above the others in society. His was a loftier vocation; he had special graces to live a holy life; he was held up as an example of Christ's presence in the world. In the post-Vatican II era, this higher vocation has been dismantled. Priests, as well as other public figures, have been placed under close public scrutiny and have been found wanting. "Pride goeth before the fall." To be exalted in the public eye is to be set up for a great fall.

In this era of "the great fall," the self-image of priests and religious has plummeted. There is an often unspoken assumption: "Only someone with a multitude of personal and psychological problems would want to minister in the church." Before, we felt as if we were the best; now, we secretly fear that we are among the worst.

In a study of the psychological health of U. S. Catholic priests conducted in the 1970s, there were four levels of development that the 271 participants were evaluated against: maldeveloped, underdeveloped, developing, and developed (Kennedy and Heckler, 1972). The clergy did not fare well. The great majority of priests fell into the category of emotionally underdeveloped (179). The next largest category was developing (50) and a few fell into the extremes of developed (19) or maldeveloped (23). It was not a pretty picture.

But the researchers noted that "priests reflect the problems of the general population." In their clinical experience, they believed that if one compared this group of priests with other males across the country, they would not fare badly. "Priests do not emerge as seriously disturbed, rebellious, or atypical individuals." In fact, the researchers found them to be "bright, able and dedicated." They noted, however, that priests suffer from the "great expectations" placed upon them. The study summarized their findings with one simple insight: "The priests of the United States are ordinary men."

This is perhaps the most important insight that every priest or religious, as well as every member of humanity, has to come to know and to accept. We are not better than others, nor are we any worse. Neither poles are productive nor healthy, and there is more than a touch of self-absorption in both. In reality, we are simply human.

A young priest is first enthralled with his ministry and, I suspect, overwhelmed by the prestige and authority that come with the position. Nothing he does goes unnoticed. Today, there is much more hostility than in former days but this, too, is a type of authority and "negative" prestige. He is noticed; he is different; people react to him in a powerful way, positively or negatively.

But then, there comes a time when the priest is faced with his limitations. He cannot see every family. He cannot be good at everything. He cannot meet his own expectations, or those of others. He is too limited and too mortal to meet such demands. How a priest responds to this "crisis of expectation" will say much about his future as a minister. And this "crisis of expectation" is not simply an event for priests or religious. It is a problem that all people face.

One psychiatrist hypothesized that the distance between the mask we present to the world and how we truly feel inside is the measure of the anxiety under which we live. The greater the distance between the expectations we have of ourselves and the reality under which we live, the greater the tension in our psychic lives. To come to grips with reality and to let go of the mask that hides our inner selves is a task that we all share. It is a task of being human.

Erik Erikson suggested that this "task of being human" involves a process of development. He said that at each stage of life, one is confronted with challenges and tasks to accomplish so that one can move on to a fuller human life. For example, the adolescent is challenged to find an "identity" and, thus, to know his or her place in the world and who he or she really is. At the end of the life cycle, Erikson posited the existence of a particular insight which would summarize the final stage of growth. It is in this awareness that we find our final liberation and our true potential. The insight is: "humankind, my kind."

In the end, we are to come to know that we are merely human. In such a knowledge there is freedom from unreal expectations and we sense a bond with all our brothers and sisters. The spiritual ramifications of such an awareness are clear. In being human, we discard the arrogance of trying to be God. In accepting our limitations and sins, we are humbled. In recognizing that we are truly human, we feel a unity in the entire Body of Christ. And where there was anxiety, there is now an inner peace.

Time for a Professional Study

The sexual abuse of children in our society and in our church—by persons who have not found inner peace—is a horrible reality. We should thank the media for raising our consciousness. It was their mission and they did it well. But the time has come to take this problem out of the media and to place it in the hands of those who will look at it in more depth and with a trained eye.

In this study, we have gathered professional people to begin the task. There is gathered here the expertise of a psychiatrist, several psychologists, a social worker, a bishop, a priest-civil lawyer, a member of the media, plus the personal witnesses of a priest-child molester and a victim of sexual abuse. Each professional is an expert in some aspect of child sexual abuse in the church. Each person provides a piece of the puzzle so that we might see the larger picture.

I feel a great sense of gratitude for them, not only for their contribution to this volume, but also for their efforts in helping our church to come to recognize her humanity in a responsible and Christ-like way. Their ministries of healing, and the professionalism and care with which these ministries are carried out, bode well for our future.

As the story of child sexual abuse unfolds, we will likely feel shocked and outraged that such horrible things should ever take place. We may also feel compassion and sadness when presented with the realities of such serious and debilitating mental illnesses. It is my hope that these emotions will spur us to take vigorous yet reasoned action to confront these difficult truths. It is as wrong to respond impulsively as it is to do nothing.

It is also my hope that we will come to recognize our common, though flawed, humanity. Such an awareness would release us from the anxious prison of unreal expectations. We are, after all, no better than our fellow men and women; we are also no worse. We are simply human. It is an easy truth to speak but a difficult one to make our own. There are few tasks more difficult. But this is the only path that will steer us clear of the Scylla of arrogance and the Charybdis of shame. And it is the only path that will save the church and our society from disintegrating under the painful reality of the sexual abuse of children.

References

Abel, G., J. Becker, M. Mittelman, J. Cunningham-Rathner, J. Rouleau and W. Murphy. "Self-reported Sex Crimes of Nonincarcerated Paraphiliacs." *Journal of Interpersonal Violence.* 1987, 2:3–25.

Kennedy, Eugene C. and Victor J. Heckler. *The Catholic Priest in the United States: Psychological Investigations.* Washington, D.C.: United States Catholic Conference, 1972.

"Former Priest Given Suspended Sentence." *Kitchener-Waterloo Record.* Kitchener, Ontario: October 19, 1989.

Myths of the Child Molester

Rev. Stephen J. Rossetti, D.Min.
L. M. Lothstein Ph.D., ABPP

Myth #1: Child Molesters Are Dirty Old Men
The popular image of the child molester is a dirty old man who stalks dark places and snatches children off the street. The underlying theme of such a portrait of the sex offender is that he is someone unlike us. While he is old, dirty, and furtive, we view ourselves as young, clean, and open to the world. All of us, including real child molesters, want to distance ourselves as far as possible from the most heinous of human impulses—to touch a child sexually.

Our Western world is outraged by child sexual abuse. For centuries, its existence was so unthinkable that it was not even admitted into our conscious thought. No one believed that children were telling the truth when they said, "Daddy did something funny with me." Sigmund Freud himself rejected his own initial hypothesis about the reality of sexual abuse and its contribution to hysteria among women. We are appalled and outraged by the mere thought of such actions. It may be, however, that in the darkest recesses of our own psyches, there are impulses not so different from the impulses of the sex offender.

Perhaps it is because it is so difficult for us to admit the presence of such dark impulses in ourselves that we cannot and will not tolerate its presence in the world. This is a *reaction formation.* To defend against admitting our own darkest side, we vociferously destroy any hint of it in the world around us. In our society, who is lower than a child molester? Even in prisons where the lowest of society are caged, the pedophile is despised.

The demographics of child abusers paint a different picture. They are not so different from us. For example, child abusers are often close friends of the family of their victims. For thirteen years a supermarket meat cutter and his family were friends of the Bronikowskis. Their families were inseparable: they went on picnics together; they remodeled their homes together; they were the closest of friends. There were clues that something was amiss but no one paid attention to them. The meat cutter, a man in his thirties, told Mr. Bronikowski, "I love your daughter more than you'll ever know." He "seemed to want to be with the kids, not the grown ups" and their 10-year-old daughter's personality began to change. Her grades dropped and she became sullen and withdrawn. The Bronikowskis never suspected that their best friend was sexually involved with their daughter (Elliott, 1989).

Interestingly, approximately 75–80 percent of abusers are well known to their victims. They may become surrogate father figures, especially in families where the father is absent, either physically or emotionally. The child molester may slowly, either consciously or unconsciously, "groom" the child. The adult gains the trust and confidence of the youth over a period of time and may desensitize the child to sexual advances through lewd jokes, sexual innuendoes, and inappropriate touching and hugging. The notion of a dirty old stranger who suddenly whisks a child away in a dark alley is a stereotypical—and inaccurate—portrait of most sex offenders.

In fact, most molesters are a lot like us. Child abusers, for example, are usually not old men. The Kinsey study found that the median age at first conviction for pedophiles was 34.5 years for heterosexuals and 30.2 for homosexuals (Bancroft, 1989). Most began to abuse children at a much younger age. Lanyon (1986) points out that "the child molester is most commonly a respectable, otherwise law-abiding person, who may escape detection for exactly that reason." Abel *et al.* (1987) reported that sexual deviations, including pedophilia, are "found in all sectors of society." The average child molester is a man who is young, well-educated, middle-class, married, Caucasian (61%), and employed in a stable job at a good salary. In fact, one study using slides of naked children found "many men" with no reported history of child abuse nor sexual interest in children becoming sexually aroused by the slides (Freund, 1972).

By convention we use the pronoun "he" to refer to child molesters. Are they always men? At this point in our society, approximately 90 percent of the known child molesters are men. No doubt there are many proposed reasons for this. It is sometimes thought that men in our society tend to *externalize* their psychic conflicts while women tend to *internalize* them. Thus, men who were abused as youths have a higher probability of themselves becoming abusers or acting out their psychic trauma in violent actions and other external ways. Women, on the other hand, are more likely to internalize the trauma and become depressed, engage in eating disorders and/or become suicidal.

Public awareness and reporting of child abuse, however, has only recently begun. As hard as it was for us to admit that men are sexually abusing young girls and boys, it may be equally as difficult to accept that mothers abuse their own children. Simply, we may not want to admit it. It is also easier for a mother in our society to disguise inappropriate contact with youngsters as maternal acts of cleaning, grooming and dressing.

In a similar vein, societal prejudices affect our ability to acknowledge the sexual abuse of teenage boys by older women. In a movie that spawned the term, "Summer of '42 Phenomenon," a teenage boy had a sexual encounter with a woman 10 years older. This encounter was sometimes called a "score" for the boy or a "coming of age" event. However, if the person had been a man and the teenager had been a girl, we would have called it statutory rape and sexual abuse. Such cognitive distortions in our entire society limit our ability to know the truth.

Myth #2: All Child Molesters Are Homosexual

In a recent workshop for a religious community, the community's vocation director stated that they are no longer accepting homosexuals as candidates for their order. When asked the reason, the vocation director responded, "Because of all this pedophilia stuff that is going on." In a similar instance, Rev. Andrew Greeley, writing in the November 10, 1989 issue of the *National Catholic Reporter*, claimed that "Most homosexuals, it should be noted, are not pedophiles and some pedophiles are not homosexual. Nonetheless, the two phenomena shade into one another." The implication in both these examples is that a homosexual orientation predisposes a person to abusing children and/or that homosexuals are the ones who are committing these acts of child abuse.

The list of studies which refute such implications is long. For example, Groth and Birnbaum (1978) concluded that "homosexuality and homosexual pedophilia may be mutually exclusive and that the adult heterosexual male constitutes a greater risk to the underage child than does the adult homosexual male." Freund *et al.* (1984) reported that the development of pedophilia and either heterosexuality or homosexuality were independent of each other. Abel *et al.* (1987) also suggested that homosexual men posed a lesser risk to children and teens than did heterosexual men. In fact, most known child abusers in the United States are heterosexual males such as fathers, stepfathers, cousins, uncles or older brothers who sexually abuse girls in their own families.

Bancroft (1989) in *Human Sexuality and Its Problems* stated that "the majority of pedophiles marry at some stage." While this does not mean they are exclusively heterosexuals, it would appear from such a statement that many, if not most, pedophiles appear to be attracted to the opposite sex. What Bancroft notes is not so much the sexual orientation of the offender, but that pedophiles have problems in "establishing satisfactory adult relationships."

One mother of four children who was married to a pedophile complained that she had to take care of *five* children: her four offspring and her husband. The pedophile related to his wife as a son to his mother. Marital breakdowns are not uncommon for pedophiles. Bancroft's observations suggest that an inability to engage in satisfying close relationships with peers may be a more important factor than one's sexual orientation in contributing to child sexual molestation.

In working at the Institute for Living, Dr. Lothstein notes that many child sexual abusers would identify themselves as heterosexual, even if they had been involved with children of the same sex, and genuinely appeared to be so. For most of us, this seems to be a contradiction. If, for example, a man is accused of molesting a young boy, would he not necessarily be a homosexual? Sometimes he is a homosexual, but this is not always the case. Other times, heterosexual men molest boys. This appears to be especially true of priests and religious.

It appears that a variety of factors can inhibit priests' healthy acknowledgment of their heterosexual interests, enabling them to refocus their sexual interests on the male child. For example, many priest child molesters confess to growing up in a repressive environment which subtly, or not so subtly, told them to "stay away from girls" or that "sexual desires concerning women are evil." While the priest might be heterosexual, he believes it is wrong even to feel his sexual attraction to women. He becomes extremely threatened by his own heterosexual feelings.

Ironically, no one ever told them it was wrong to have a sexual encounter with boys. Many priest sex offenders report not hearing the same negative message about sex with boys. When they reached puberty, they began to have sexual feelings and said that they knew it was wrong to be with girls but it seemed okay to have an encounter with their male friends. And no one put a stop to it. They grew up with a belief that sex with boys is okay.

In such cases, sexual abusers who are priests or religious may report that a physical encounter with a boy is not really sex and thus is not truly evil. While this rationalization is an example of defending oneself against a painful truth, it also suggests a distortion that was fostered from an early age: sex with women is the ultimate sin; therefore, sex with boys is a lesser sin.

Moreover, a sexual encounter with a woman is often perceived as a fundamental threat to a celibate vocation. If a priest allows himself to experience this desire, he believes it will challenge his entire vocation and threaten his priestly existence. In fact, some will say, "I only break my celibacy vows if I have sex with a woman." For those who over-identify with their religious vocations and have a tenuous sense of self, this would be seen as a threat to their self-image and personal identity. Such a threat is so fundamental that it would be repelled at all costs.

Some may even admit that a sexual relationship with a boy is wrong and sinful, but they add, "I can confess this sin, be forgiven, and start my life all over again." An encounter with a woman is not dealt with in such a facile manner. It is perceived as a challenge to their core identity. With such a distorted view of celibacy and sexuality, their entire cognitive world would be destroyed by such a heterosexual experience. Not surprisingly, then, our clinical experience to date points out that it is very rare to find a priest or religious who molests girls, regardless of the perpetrator's innate sexual preference.

As D. Newton (1978) concluded after his review of the research on this issue, "Existing studies...provide no reason to believe that anything other than a random connection exists between homosexual behavior and child molestation." Homosexuality and child abuse are two different realities that spring from two different psychodynamic sets of factors. Homosexuality is probably as closely linked to pedophilia as heterosexuality is to rape. One should question whether the tendency to lay the blame on the homosexual population for child molestation is not a case of societal homophobia and an attempt to shift the focus away from where it should be—on ourselves.

Myth #3: All Child Molesters are Pedophiles
During a clinical interview with a priest convicted of sexually molesting children, the priest identified himself as a pedophile. The children he had molested ranged in age from 15–17—all had passed the stage of puberty. Apparently, his original therapist had named him a pedophile and his diocese and brother priests had likewise labeled him one. This man, however, was not a pedophile.

Pedophilia is a specific psychiatric diagnosis. It is listed as a mental disorder in the psychologist's "bible" entitled the Diagnostic and Statistical Manual (DSM). (Now in its third recently revised edition, it is called the DSM-III-R.) Pedophilia is defined as "recurrent intense sexual urges and sexually arousing fantasies involving sexual activity with a *prepubescent* child" (italics added).

The pedophile's object of sexual desire is a child who has not yet reached puberty. The pedophile may fantasize about having sexual encounters with children, and the mere thought of a child can be sexually stimulating. Such a disordered sexuality is indeed a serious mental illness. It is often accompanied by other mental aberrations such as depression, an inadequate personality, and other sexual deviations such as exhibitionism and voyeurism. The prognosis for a true pedophile is not bright. Although their sexual behavior can be controlled, the underlying sexual arousal by children is thought to be intractable.

Child sexual abuse in the church is often thought to be a problem of pedophilia. Actually, it has more to do with a problem called ephebophilia. The news carries stories of priests, religious, and other church personnel who are involved with children in their teens such as altar boys and high school youth groups members. Though these child molesters are called pedophiles, they are not. They are, rather, ephebophiles for they are sexually involved with postpubescent children. It is an important distinction.

Ephebophilia is not listed in the DSM-III-R because being attracted to teenagers, of itself, is not considered to be a mental illness. Teenagers are adults, physically speaking, and, in earlier days of our culture, were married shortly after reaching their sexual maturity. Physically, they are sexually appealing and potentially arousing for another adult, regardless of the adult's age. For example, a man came in to see a priest a few years ago and was markedly upset. When the priest asked him his problem, the man said he was upset because he found the girlfriends of his teenage daughter to be sexually attractive. He was in all respects a well-adjusted man and there was no hint that any irresponsible activity had, or would, take place. He was simply upset by his sexual feelings. When the priest told him that it was natural for him to be attracted to women, even if they were socially inappropriate mates, the man relaxed.

Likewise, it would not be unusual for a homosexual male to be attracted to adolescent boys, for they too could appear physically appealing. However, a distinguishing sign of the healthy adult male is the ability to manage his sexual desires and to express them appropriately based on societal and religious values. Neither society nor our intellects, however, can tell us whom we feel sexually attracted to and to whom we do not. What we can do is control and express these desires in a morally responsible way. The adult who becomes involved with teenage men or women does not do this and thus is guilty of a crime against our society.

What is usually the case is that the actual sexual contact with an adolescent is the result of other types of mental problems which result in an inability to form close relationships with peers and a breakdown of one's social inhibitions against being involved with youths. Such pathology can become so powerful that it leads to a feeling of being out of control. It may function like an addiction.

The priest who was previously interviewed would be called an ephebophile because the children he molested were in their teens (15 to 17 years old). His actual attraction to adolescents would not be considered, in itself, pathological. However, during the course of the interview, the priest revealed that he himself had been molested by an adult beginning when he was 15 years old and lasting until he was 17. His early psychosexual trauma and later immaturity made teens appear to be suitable partners. His consequent loneliness, work-related stress, alcohol consumption and depression made him vulnerable and even "driven" by his sexual impulses. What was not really a problem of deviant sexual desires ended up in a destructive sexual encounter.

While there are no statistics available, we would estimate that over 90 percent of priests and religious who sexually molest children are not true pedophiles. They are involved with postpubertal adolescents; they are therefore ephebophiles.

Myth #4: Child Molesters Can Never Be Returned to Ministry
There is a debate in the church whether child molesters can be returned to ministry. However, many would be surprised to know that more than a few priests and other church personnel who have admitted to child abuse have already been successfully returned to ministry. The question is not so much "if" they should return to ministry but "which ones" should return and the guidelines by which we implement reintegration.

Specific clinical and legal guidelines are suggested in later chapters of this book, but any discussion of the long-term outlook of the child molester should include a diagnosis of the underlying problem. Is the person a pedophile or an ephebophile? All things being equal, the prognosis for ephebophiles is better than for pedophiles.

It is rare to find a true pedophile in the priesthood or religious life. Most priest or religious child abusers, while having significant psychic problems, are not pedophiles and often respond well to treatment. The experience among the residential treatment centers is that these child sex abusers can be treated effectively. The priest who was interviewed has not been sexually involved with children after a lengthy stay in a qualified residential treatment facility and after an equally rigorous, long-term follow-up program. He has re-entered society and has again become a productive member of his community. His case is not unusual.

However, when speaking of the abusers of prepubescent children, i.e., authentic pedophiles, their fixated, intense, sexual attraction to these young children is a more serious mental disorder. There is little thought of changing their deviant pattern of arousal; they are likely always to remain sexually excited by young children. What is hoped for is a containment of their sexual behavior. Barring any extreme measures such as castration, the likelihood of recidivism is high enough to cause one to question the possibility of returning them to a position of public trust. This could change, however, with future advances in the clinical treatment of pedophiles.

Child sexual abuse is a complex phenomenon, involving much more than a single, clinical diagnosis. Within the categories of pedophilia and ephebophilia there are as many personalities as there are people. We recommend that considerations of returning someone to active ministry include a separate look at each individual case. While no decision to return someone can ever be free of risk, it can be based on sound clinical judgment, informed legal advice, and the best pastoral guidelines available.

The contract between bishop/religious superior and one who ministers in his or her jurisdiction is never without its risks. The one who ministers is obliged to build up the Kingdom of God and to do so without causing scandal and damaging the good name and work of the superior and other ministers. The superior, on the other hand, is obliged to provide the pastoral care and support necessary for the person and the ministry. There are times when both parties do not live up to the unspoken agreement.

The case of the minister who abuses children is most serious because of the enormous scandal and the devastation it causes among the people involved and, indeed, within the wider church. Because of this issue's volatility and its relatively recent emergence, the church is scrambling for a perspective on the situation and guidelines for a measured response. As has been suggested, there are many erroneous myths, usually a mixture of fact and fiction, concerning who the child molester is and how he or she should be treated.

As a society, we would like to believe that child molesters are different, perhaps even evil, and that they should be treated with contempt and removed from our midst. Indeed, their crimes cannot be minimized, but neither can our common, broken humanity. We must not forget our own inner darkness which makes us resemble the "dirty old man" that stalks his prey in the night. The existence of our private darkness frightens us just as much as the specter of the active child molester. Perhaps if we are afraid of this "dirty old man," concoct unreal myths about him, and wish to banish him from our midst, it is because we are afraid of what he shows us about ourselves. But the truth is he is in our midst, and he looks a lot like us.

References

Abel, G., J. Becker, M. Mittelman, J. Cunningham-Rathner, J. Rouleau and W. Murphy. "Self-Reported Sex Crimes of Nonincarcerated Paraphiliacs." *Journal of Interpersonal Violence*. 1987, 2:3–25.

American Psychiatric Association. *Diagnostic and Statistical Manual of Mental Disorders, Revised (DSM-III-R)*, Washington, D.C.: APA Press, 1987.

Bancroft, John. *Human Sexuality and Its Problems*. London: Churchill Livingstone, 1989.

Elliott, Julia. "Mom of Abused Girl Becomes Crusader." *The Ottawa Citizen*. Ottawa, Ontario: October 17, 1989.

Freund, K., C. McKnight, R. Langevin and S. Cibiri. "The Female Child As a Surrogate Object." *Archives of Sexual Behavior*. 1972, 2:119–133.

Freund, K., G. Heasma, I. Racansky and G. Glancy. "Pedophilia and Heterosexuality vs. Homosexuality." *Journal of Sex and Marital Therapy*. 1984, 10:193–200.

Groth, N. and H. Birnbaum. "Adult Sexual Orientation and Attraction to Underage Persons." *Archives of Sexual Behavior*. 1978, 7:175–181.

Lanyon, R. "Theory and Treatment in Child Molestation," *Journal of Consulting and Clinical Psychology*. 1986, 54:176–182.

Newton, D. "Homosexual Behavior and Child Molestation." *Adolescence*. 1978, 13:29–43.

Psychological Theories
of Pedophilia and Ephebophilia

L.M. Lothstein, Ph.D., ABPP

Prelude
After 35 years of sexually molesting prepubescent male children, John (a pseudonym) was finally arrested. An intense but friendly man, John betrayed those who trusted him the most. All of his victims were his friends' children. He had no remorse. He was so excited by children that he became sexually aroused when he heard their footsteps or their voices. Just before his arrest, John planned to abduct and murder a male child at random. The idea of lust-murder excited him. Prior to his indictment, he presented me with the following poem he wrote which captures the aggression and rage in the child molester's motivation for sexually exploiting children.

I am the slayer of the soul
   destroyer of the dream
The nightmares which recur
   and wake you with your screams.

I am the end of innocence
   the planting of the fear

That eats away inside your mind
and kills you year by year.

I am the words you cannot speak
and acts that you regret
The twisted childhood memories
that you cannot forget.

I am the terror in your voice
as painfully you plea
To fight the urges inside of you
to end up just like me.

At 55 years of age, John was a professional, an individual who
earned the respect of his colleagues. They were shocked when
they learned of his deceptions. He was charged with over 200
counts of child sexual abuse over a 35-year period. How, one
might ask, can such a thing happen?

Introduction
The clinical evaluation of pedophiles reveals them to be a diverse
group. They differ educationally, vocationally, religiously, and so-
cio-economically. They vary in the amount of force or aggression
used in their pedophilic acts. They may be involved in a wide variety of other variant sexual behaviors, called paraphilias, such as
exhibitionism, voyeurism, frotteurism (sexually touching or fondling an unwilling person), masochism or sadism (Money, 1984).
Also, they vary in the many different causes that led to the development of their sexual problems.

For some child molesters, their sexual acting out can be explained by the presence of a psychosis or an organic brain deficit.
Individuals with a history of closed or open head injuries and
individuals with a diagnosis of schizophrenia may become
sexually aggressive because of their unique mental disorder or
because of their brain injuries. For example, there is a group of
brain damaged individuals who molest children because of a
prior head injury or impaired intellectual functioning. Their
pedophilic behavior is not the result of a primary sexual disorder
but of an organic disorder.

Thus, no single explanation can account for all the different
pathways leading towards pedophilia. Any theory of pedophilia

must be multifaceted and account for the wide range of behaviors, fantasies, and organic factors that may play a role in the development of this disorder. A comprehensive theory of pedophilia must refer to psychological, familial, environmental, so-˙ cial, genetic, hormonal, organic, and biological factors.

Distinctions

Any discussion of the causes of the sexual abuse of children should distinguish between *pedophila* and *ephebophila*. A *pedophile*, as mentioned in the previous chapter, is an adult who has recurrent, intense, sexual urges and sexually arousing fantasies involving a prepubescent child. The age of the child is arbitrarily set at 13 years or younger and the adult is at least 5 years older than the child. An *ephebophile* is an adult who has recurrent, intense sexual urges and sexually arousing fantasies but whose object is a pubescent child or adolescent. The age of the child is arbitrarily set at 14 through 17 years. Again, the adult is at least 5 years older than is the child.

A distinction made by Groth, Hobson, and Gary (1982) is significant. They divided pedophiles into two groups, *regressed* and *fixated*. *Regressed* pedophiles were described as individuals with a primary sexual orientation toward adults of the opposite sex. Under conditions of extreme stress, the regressed pedophile may psychologically regress to an earlier psychosexual age and engage in sex with children. The typical case is a male whose wife is emotionally unavailable to him and who thus turns to his daughter for sex. *Fixated* pedophiles/ephebophiles have a primary sexual interest in children or teens; they rarely, if ever, engage in sex with peers. In most cases, they are described as exclusively interested in children or teenagers.

A Four-Factor Approach

In a review of the research, Araji and Finkelhor (1985) raise several critical questions that must be answered:

1. Why does the adult have an emotional need to relate to children?

2. Why does the adult become sexually aroused by children?

3. Why are alternative sources of sexual and emotional gratification not available?

4. Why can the adult not inhibit arousal toward children/teens based on normal prohibitions against sexual behavior with minors?

Their review suggested that 1) children have a special meaning to pedophiles because of the children's lack of dominance (emotional congruence); 2) pedophiles have an "unusual pattern of sexual arousal toward children" (deviant sexual arousal); 3) pedophiles seem "blocked in their social and heterosexual relationships" (blockage); and 4) many pedophiles were sexually abused as children, and use alcohol or other drugs to lower their inhibitions prior to offending with children (disinhibition).

Araji and Finkelhor then view the theories of pedophilia as organized into these four basic categories: emotional congruence, sexual arousal, blockage, and disinhibition. Any perspective on pedophilia/ephebophilia will have to address this four factor approach and the regressed-fixated typology presented by Groth, Hobson, and Gary (1982).

The following cases are presented in order to address the four questions raised by Araji and Finkelhor, to demonstrate differences within groups of pedophiles and ephebophiles, and to illustrate the problems in diagnosis. Some of these cases have individuals whose sexual behavior is the result of severe mental illness (e.g., schizophrenia, psychosis) or because of organic disorders. Individuals who sexually act out with children or teenagers because of a severe emotional or organic pathology should not be diagnosed as having a *primary* psychosexual disorder. A recognition of these diagnostic difficulties is important for arriving at a theory of pedophilia.

These cases highlight the distinction between the fixated and the regressed pedophile or ephebophile. In reviewing each of the following vignettes, the reader should consider what it means to call someone a pedophile or ephebophile and what additional questions need to be posed for each individual case.

Clinical Cases

Case 001: Mr. B. is a 36-year-old married man who was sexually addicted to adult pornography, prostitutes, and cruising. He was arrested while exposing himself and masturbating in his car. Recently, he became obsessed with the idea that in order to be accepted by his sexually deviant friends he would have to try everything. This is his explanation for becoming incestuously involved with his 5-year-old daughter and his 14-month-old son. His wife was unaware of his sexual acting out. As a child, she had been sexually molested by her father and uncle and she had been raped by a stranger. Mr. B. lacked an appreciation of what effect his behavior had on his children and viewed his behavior as impulsive and self-gratifying, but within normal limits.

Comments: This man's hypersexuality was controlled by drugs (lithium and depo-provera) and psychotherapeutic interventions. In addition to a compulsive sexual disorder, he was also diagnosed as having a manic-depressive disorder. His pedophilia was considered to be "regressed," precipitated by stress and the onset of his manic-depressive psychosis. He was primarily heterosexual and denied any homosexual orientation. Alcohol and drugs fueled his sexual addiction and lowered his inhibitions against acting out. His incestuous behavior was part of a pattern of uncontrolled sexuality and he would not receive a primary diagnosis of pedophilia.

> **Case 002:** Mr. C., a 35-year-old computer programmer, worked in a rural part of the country. He spent most of his time fantasizing about having sex with either boys or girls. He bribed his victims with toys, money, and attention. His modus operandi was to get close to the parents and involve himself with the children in a way that relieved the parents of their daily responsibilities with their children and of having to cope with their children's negative emotions. Mr. C. performed oral, anal, and vaginal sex on his victims. He had no understanding of how his behavior frightened the children. His thinking was grossly impaired, though he did not have a formal thought disorder. Mr. C. had poor social skills and could not relate in an appropriate way to peers.

Comments: Mr. C. is a "fixated" pedophile who is exclusively interested in children. He has an inadequate personality and is grossly immature, developmentally arrested, and psychosexually naive. He is a lonely, withdrawn individual who denies any sexual interest in teenagers or adults.

> **Case 003:** Ms. K. was a 19-year-old student who, while babysitting, fondled and masturbated a 5-year-old girl. This was not the only child she molested....When she herself was 5 years old, Ms. K. herself had been sexually molested by her

baby sitter. She had no insight into the effect that molestation
had on her. She used her babysitting jobs to procure girls for
sexual exploitation. A socially immature and overweight
woman, Ms. K. came from a chaotic family environment in
which her father was having an affair with her boyfriend's
mother. Ms. K. was primarily sexually aroused toward boys
her age and had been sexually active with her boyfriend.
Since age 15 she had a chronic drug and alcohol addiction.

Comments: Ms. K.'s sexual acting out with children was regressed and occasioned by the anniversary of her own sexual exploitation at age 5. She was primarily heterosexual but felt drawn
to fondle and masturbate very young girls. During the fondling
and masturbation, she felt aroused and masturbated herself. She
used drugs and alcohol to disinhibit herself and "feel good."

Case 004: Mr. D. was a 38-year-old Protestant minister who
arranged for teenage boys to have sex with his wife so that
he could watch, become aroused, and masturbate. Eventually, he participated in the "sexual arrangement" and performed oral and anal sex on the boys. Victims were pro-
cured through social agencies that placed delinquent
adolescents in foster homes. Using his ministerial creden-
tials, he served as a foster parent who then seduced the boys
into perverse sexual practices. He was only interested in vulnerable teenage boys who had nothing to lose. No drugs or
alcohol were used. In some instances, pictures were taken
that were later used by Mr. D. to bribe the boys to maintain
their silence.

Comments: Mr. D. is a sexual predator with bisexual interests fo-
cusing on adult women and teenage boys. He uses his ministerial
role to overpower the boys and coerce them into deviant sexual
practices. His paraphilic behavior includes voyeurism, ephebophilia, troilism (sex involving three people), and compulsive masturbation. His primary excitement focuses on sex with teenage
boys; his heterosexual activity with his wife serves merely as a
screen for his real interest.

Case 005: Fr. W. was a 35-year-old diocesan priest referred
for treatment because of several allegations of sexually abusing teenage boys. Over the course of eight years, he had sex-

ually abused more than two dozen boys ranging in age from 13 to 16. All of the boys were either under his supervision as altar servers or ones he met through church-related programs. He was known as someone who was gifted in his ability to work with teenagers. Typically, he would choose a boy who appealed to him and then plan to seduce him by inviting him for pizza, a movie or video, or taking him on an outing. Eventually he engaged the boys in mutual masturbation and oral sex.

Of particular concern was the fact that Fr. W. was becoming more self-absorbed in his ephebophilic interests, preoccupied by sexual fantasies of seducing boys, and masturbating more than three times a day. In therapy, he talked about his need for the boys to admire him and put him on a pedestal. He had no awareness of how his role as priest exerted a powerful influence over the boys and how they were harmed by his behavior.

Comments: Fr. W. was a fixated ephebophile. He had an exclusive sexual interest in teenage boys and viewed his primary friendships as being with teenagers. He presented a pattern of disinhibition, emotional congruence with teenage boys, sexual arousal to teenage boys, and a lack of interest in heterosexual relationships and age-appropriate relationships. Because of his narcissistic needs and sociopathic tendencies, treatment was very difficult and he remained at high risk for further acting out.

Investigative Questions
After reviewing the previous clinical vignettes, the following are examples of the questions that might be addressed when investigating each case:
- Is the sexual interest directed to a prepubescent or pubescent child?
- Is the disorder fixated or regressed?
- What is the level of ego functioning of the individual?
- How does the individual handle stress? frustration? loneliness?
- How much aggression is involved?
- Is she/he capable of relating to adult males? to adult females?
- Does the individual have another primary DSM III-R diagnosis that can explain the behavior?

• Is the individual capable of empathizing with the child's pain?
• Has the person been sexually abused as a child or overstimulated by sexual events?
• Are there other family members with similar problems?
• Is the individual psychosexually and/or psychosocially developmentally arrested?
• Is there evidence of self-esteem?
• What role did pornography play in the person's psychosexual development?
• Are there unresolved Oedipal dynamics?
• Is there an attempt to master early childhood trauma through repetition (i.e., repetition compulsion)?
• Are there cultural or religious norms which support the individual's sexual deviancy?
• What role do drugs and alcohol play in fueling the behavior?

This is not an exhaustive list, but it is representative of the questions that need to be answered in order to understand the dynamics of each case.

These vignettes point to the heterogeneity and complexity of pedophilia/ephebophilia. Essentially, we may be dealing with a number of disorders, one symptom of which is the sexual exploitation of children or teenagers. Some clinicians have even suggested that the sexual symptom may be the first indicator of an organic brain disease.

The remainder of this chapter will divide our investigation of the causes of pedophilia/ephebophilia into two basic areas: 1) psychological theories including psychic, social, and environmental factors; and 2) the hypothesized biological substrata of the disorder.

Psychological Theories of Pedophilia/Ephebophilia

Psychological theories address only those aspects of the emotional congruence, sexual arousal, blockage, and disinhibition found in pedophilia and ephebophilia that are independent of organic causes. These theories include such diverse perspectives as psychoanalysis, social learning theory, and family systems. While I have argued that a single perspective cannot explain the complex phenomena of pedophilia and ephebophilia, this does not mean that psychological theories are irrelevant. Rather, an integrated approach that combines several different perspectives is recommended.

Psychoanalytic theories look at deviant sexual behavior as stemming from early childhood trauma during years 2 to 5. This trauma, which may take the form of sexual or physical abuse, leaves the child in a state of overstimulation, confusion, separation anxiety, and rage. Feeling helpless, out of control, and powerless, this victim may, in turn, sexually act out as a way of re-creating the original trauma and attempting to master the anxiety associated with it. This psychic mechanism is called a repetition compulsion.

Or, this victim may identify with the aggressor, that is, he or she may identify with the abusing adult and then act out sexually with a younger child. Identifying with the aggressor would enable the person to defend against the unwanted feelings of helplessness and powerlessness. The sexual acting out with children or adolescents makes the individual feel alive and vital; it re-establishes a feeling of control, dominance, and power, and allays the anxiety associated with the childhood trauma.

However, this is only an illusory feeling of having solved an earlier childhood conflict. The feelings of dominance, control, power, and being alive soon dissipate and the re-enactment (i.e., the molestation) has to be repeated. Because the molester's attempts at mastery and problem-solving are illusory, he/she must molest over and over again. It is only through psychological treatment and intervention that the sexual behavior can be brought under control.

The following case illustrates this point:

> *Fr. J. was raised by an alcoholic mother who was seduced by, and who slept with, the parish priest who slipped into her bed under the watchful eyes of her young (presumably asleep) son. Later in life, he was physically abused and sexually humiliated by a group of priests in a boarding school. Eventually, when he became a priest, he found himself targeting adolescent boys for sexual experiences and re-enacting his early childhood trauma by sexually abusing them.*

The repetition compulsion and identification with the aggressor were central elements to Fr. J.'s sexual behavior.

Psychoanalytic theories regard pedophilia as resulting from arrested emotional development between the ages of 2 to 5 years old. Because of the unresolved feelings associated with the childhood trauma, he or she may eventually become the offending

adult who compulsively repeats the pedophilic act with others in
an attempt to master the original anxiety. This compulsion to repeat has come to be known as the addictive process in pedophilia.

Family system theories stress the role of unresolved intergenerational
family dynamics on specific family members. Litin *et al.* (1956) have
argued that deviant sexuality is learned within the family. It first
arises within the nuclear family and then is unconsciously transmitted along family lines. Thus, individual members can be "targeted" to act out family conflicts (Lothstein, 1983, 1989).

For example, an unconscious conflict which is unacceptable to
a parent may be encouraged in a child. A parent's unconscious
wish to act out sexually with children may be repressed or
pushed out of consciousness because of the fear of punishment.
These unresolved wishes may be projected onto a child who is
vulnerable. In the context of subtle family communications, the
child may be passively or actively encouraged to act out those parental wishes. In this way, parents can both repress the forbidden
sexual impulse and act it out through their child's behavior.

Typically, family system theories focus on communication patterns within a family and regard the sexual symptom of any one
family member as being influenced by the specific communication patterns of that family. These family patterns exercise a powerful influence on the child.

Behaviorism (Barlow and Wincze, 1980) and social learning theories
(Phillips, 1978) stress the importance of learning our behavior. For example, a child may have had same-sex experiences with other
children or adults which were prolonged. Sexual excitement, even
when it is the result of abuse, is pleasurable. Pleasure is a strong,
positive reinforcer of behavior and, thus, such sexual experiences
have a high probability of becoming learned behavior and/or of
becoming generalized to other sexual behavior.

At the same time, a child who has been sexually assaulted by
an adult or another child may experience a tremendous guilt over
these early sexual experiences. This guilt is likely to be associated
in the child's mind with sexual curiosity and sexual pleasure. The
child is thus vulnerable to distressing symptoms because of the
internal conflict of guilt versus pleasure associated with normal
sexuality. When the child becomes an adult, this internal conflict,

and the resulting ambivalence, may take the form of sexually acting out with children.

This psychological approach, stressing the psychic, social and environmental factors that give rise to child sexual molestation, must never lose sight of the importance of biological factors. These factors acknowledge the importance of organic issues, especially brain pathology.

Biological Theories of Pedophilia/Ephebophilia
The search for a biological explanation of pedophilia/ephebophilia is compelling and has attracted many researchers. The central question is: What effect does the brain have on perverse sexual behavior? Can deviant sexual arousal be attributed to brain illness or damage? This is an important question, the answer to which might link sexually deviant behavior to a brain disease. Research in this area has taken several paths, linking certain kinds of brain damage and hormonal problems to sexual deviance.

Psychologists have shown that the male sex drive and male aggression are mostly regulated by the male hormone testosterone. Researchers have inquired: Does too much of this male hormone lead to violence or chaotic and deviant sexuality? Many have suggested that there is a direct relationship between male hormone levels and aggression/sexuality, although this relationship is not a simple one.

Some studies have even shown that a fetus can be adversely affected by its mother's stress or by the specific drugs she took during pregnancy. These events may alter the testosterone levels of the fetus in utero. Researchers have speculated that specific brain pathways are created in utero by hormonal changes in the mother. Thus, the mother's hormones may have a profound effect on her fetus by organizing such diverse behavioral patterns as sexual identity and sexual orientation which are not manifested until years after birth.

Is there a relationship between hormones and pedophilia? Berlin and Coyle (1981) did find significantly elevated testosterone levels in pedophiles. Another research team (Gaffner and Berlin, 1984) found unusually elevated levels in pedophiles of another hormone called "luteinising hormone" when they were given injections of a related hormone LHRH (luteinising hormone-releasing hormone). Like testosterone, luteinising hormone and LHRH have been connected with human sexual behavior. The researchers concluded that there is a specific hormonal abnormality in many pedophiles.

Anti-androgenic medication such as depo-provera lowers the testosterone levels in the human body and has been used with some success in sexually deviant men. The medication may raise their threshold for sexually acting out, increase their capacity for handling frustration, and decrease the frequency of erotic and compulsive sexual fantasizing. The effectiveness of such anti-androgenic medication provides additional support for the existence of hormone abnormalities in some types of child sexual molesters. Though sexual behavior can be influenced by changes in the male sex hormone, abnormal levels of this hormone cannot explain why certain individuals find children sexually arousing.

Another line of research has focused on naturally occurring "experiments." Regenstein and Reich (1978) reported on four cases of men whose pedophilia began after the onset of some kind of brain injury. These men also showed cognitive impairment: their thinking was disorganized and confused. Miller *et al.* (1986) reported on eight patients in whom hypersexuality or altered sexual preference (homosexuality and/or pedophilia) occurred after brain injury such as head trauma or injuries resulting from a stroke. They concluded that "in some patients, altered sexual behavior may be the presenting or dominant feature of brain injury."

Other studies have tested groups of pedophiles using newer medical technologies that can "image" the brain (PET scans, MRI, brain imaging) and reveal specific brain abnormalities. Moreover, using neuropsychological tests, psychologists have correlated the paraphile's brain abnormality with behavioral problems. We can not only document that there is brain abnormality using sophisticated medical technology, we can also relate specific behavioral problems to specific brain deficits. And almost all of these studies have found some kind of brain abnormality or damage in pedophiles. Whatever the abnormality is, it is not due to the toxic effects of alcohol or drugs alone.

Lothstein, Cassens, and Ford (1990), using electrical activity mapping techniques and neuropsychological testing, found that the frontal and temporal parts of the brain are dysfunctional in pedophiles and in other paraphiles. Damage to the frontal part of the brain leads to disinhibition, poor judgment, anxiety, low frustration tolerance, and impulsivity. Damage to the temporal parts of the brain may lead to deviant fantasizing, compulsive thinking about sexuality, and hypersexuality. These findings suggest that pedophiles might have a brain disease which leads to deviant sexual behaviors. Again, this type of research cannot yet answer why an individual's sexual pathology takes a specific form.

There is also a relationship between alcohol, substance abuse, and the paraphilias that needs to be explored fully. Most sexually deviant men report using alcohol excessively prior to acting out sexually. The alcohol or drugs seem to lower their inhibitions while increasing their level of impulsivity. However, not all sex offenders use alcohol or drugs prior to their sexual encounters. Moreover, the use of alcohol does not explain the content, aim, and direction of a child molester's sexuality. Clearly, alcohol may fuel the fires of a pedophile's sexual desires and increase the dangers of acting out, but it does not cause pedophilia/ephebophilia. An individual with brain pathology who drinks excessively may, however, be increasing the likelihood of some kind of deviant sexual behavior occurring.

In sum, there seems to be a relationship between 1) male hormone and hyper/deviant sexuality, and 2) brain pathology and hyper/deviant sexuality. Some might even characterize the evidence as pointing to a specific kind of brain disease that can trigger acting-out behavior. Indeed, the pedophilic triad of impulsivity, poor planning, and disinhibition is not only a functional description of their deficits, but may also be descriptive of the effects of their brain dysfunction. While it is not currently possible to answer the question of whether or not biological factors organize the pedophile's behavior, it is possible to say that they help to activate those behaviors.

Some Explanations of Pedophilia and Ephebophilia

Fixated vs. Regressed   In attempting to explain *why* an individual expresses his/her sexual drive toward children or adolescents, the previously cited distinction between fixated and regressed is useful. Fixated sexual offenders direct their sexual drives only toward children or adolescents. They are not aroused by adults under any condition. In many cases, there is an exclusive interest in one sex or the other, or with a certain kind of child (e.g., blue-eyed, brown hair). Sexual offenders who indiscriminately choose children of either sex or from a variety of age groups are less likely to benefit from treatment.

Fixated pedophiles typically are:

- developmentally arrested
- psychosexually immature
- non-assertive
- heterosexually inhibited
- lacking in social skills
- without a basic knowledge of sexuality.

Fixated child molesters talk about their need for control over others and how the child can be a wonderfully pliant object to control and manipulate. Fixated child molesters are dangerous because they may become chronic sexual predators, voraciously incorporating children into their sexual lives. On the other hand, regressed child molesters may be able to control their sexual impulses once their coping skills are rehabilitated, the stimulus cues for sexually acting out are understood, and a prevention program is initiated. This is not necessarily the case for fixated child molesters. *Thus, the diagnosis of fixated or regressed is important for predicting treatment outcome.*

Fixated sexual offenders may have had early childhood sexual experiences which overstimulated them and linked their sexual interest to children. For example, one woman recalled how her son, as a child (now 28 years old), always undressed other children and played doctor. He continued playing these games through adulthood. His mother apparently cooperated by not discouraging him from carrying these childish games into his adolescence and adulthood.

In another case, a clergyman recalled how he became fixated on the penis, undressed every teenage boy he was able to, and had a compulsive desire to look at boys' genitals. Another clergyman talked about his quest for the perfect, smooth penis which he would take inside himself. These penile images and the regression to childhood games suggest that early childhood themes can become part of the fabric of adult experience.

Other psychic, social, environmental, and biological factors need to be put into place if child molestation is to occur. In order to help differentiate the motivation for sexual involvement with either children or teenagers, the following ideas may be helpful.

The Pedophile

For a pedophile, the emotional congruence factor is critical. The perpetrator is developmentally arrested and may be at the same psychosexual age as his victims. *Thus, the pedophile emotionally and sexually identifies with the child who becomes his or her victim.* Pedophiles may even engage in sexual acts appropriate to their arrested psychosexual age such as showing or touching. For example, the pedophile might say to the child, "Let me see what you have and I will show you what I have."

Power and control are critical factors for the pedophile. The child is pliant and yielding, unlike an adult who may be rigid and unyielding. The child can be coerced and brought under control through simple requests and demands; the child will yield to the adult's power and control because it stills lacks autonomy and self-initiative. If the adult is employed in a high status/powerful role (e.g, priest, teacher, coach), the child is particularly vulnerable.

The pedophile desires a sexual object that is safe and non-threatening; thus it cannot be an adult. The child is perceived as unthreatening, unaggressive, and lacking the ability to retaliate because of its small size and lack of power. In this sense, the child is not viewed by the pedophile as a real person with real needs and power.

A child is also submissive and used to bending to parental authority. By offering bribes and favors, the pedophile exercises control over the child's inner needs. In a sense, the child molester does what the adult does with the prostitute, i.e., bypasses personal autonomy and bargains via primitive economic systems. It is perhaps not a coincidence that a high percentage of prostitutes were themselves sexually abused as children.

In the pedophilic act, a sexual "game" is enacted between the perpetrator and the victim. This game may take many forms and follows the model of the "doctor" game of childhood sexual exploration. One child molester initiated contact by "wrestling" with his victims; another played a "tickling" game. A more sophisticated game involved enlisting teenage boys to complete a "sexual survey" which was then used to stimulate and excite the boys prior to the actual seduction.

For example, Father Burton was the wrestling coach at a Catholic school. Whenever he wanted to seduce a boy he would challenge him to a wrestling match and, after overpowering him, masturbate him. In another instance, John, a 25-year-old student, would spend hours researching a boy's interest and suddenly come across as "sharing" a similar interest with the boy—an interest that would lead to friendship and then sex.

The sexual excitement with a real child may defend against psychotic decompensation (i.e., "going crazy"). John, the 55-year-old professional who wrote "Slayer of the Soul" was an empty, isolated, and lonely individual who lacked any real connectedness to the social world. He lived in a fantasy realm of excitement which made him feel alive and vital, and provided him with satisfactions that were unavailable in his vocational setting. The more self-absorbed and preoccupied he became with his sexual fantasies, the more he feared going crazy and losing his mind. Acting out with children led to intense sexual excitement, feelings of exhilaration, and euphoric states which made him feel connected to the world and prevented him from becoming psychotic. In this sense, his sexual enactments with a real child were attempts to defend against an impending psychosis.

In a similar case, Chris was becoming increasingly impulsive and chaotic in his behavior. For a long time he feared he was going crazy. He had difficulty concentrating and when he spoke, he could not complete a logical train of thought. He often became confused. At times he saw things that others did not see and he heard voices. Fearing that he was going crazy, Chris found that sexual excitement made him feel alive and intact. When he exposed himself to female children at the playground, his sense of going crazy disappeared and he felt whole.

Without a real child to enact the scenario, the perpetrator may substitute an imagined child. The child molester daydreams a scenario involving a naked child or teenager. The image is sustained and the person masturbates. In some cases, the individual cannot distinguish image from reality and acts as if the child/teenager was real. Thus, such a retreat into fantasy may achieve psychotic proportions.

Jerry, a 34-year-old computer programmer, lived an isolated, lonely existence. A shy, withdrawn, aloof individual, he had poor social skills and no friends. At home he would spend hours in reveries, imaging a nude male child, and then masturbating. These hallucinated images eventually took over his entire personality as he spent 90 percent of his time imaging the boys. Eventually he was hospitalized with an acute psychosis.

In more intact individuals, sexual enactments may involve scenarios which are symbolic portrayals of early childhood traumas that they themselves had experienced. These childhood traumas are disguised and re-enacted in adult life for two reasons: 1) to identify with the aggressor; and 2) to master a childhood trauma. This repetition compulsion, a concept from psychoanalytic theory, is common to sexual offenders.

Pedophiles often state that, in order to be aroused, their victims must lack pubic hair and have a smooth body. Some pedophiles become hyperaroused by the slightest hint of a child's presence. In this sense, it is not a particular child who is arousing but the sight, smell or sounds of a child. For example, some pedophiles can only be aroused by girls with blond hair and blue eyes.

Most pedophiles (cf. Stoller, 1975), with the exception of the rare sadist, deny malevolent intent. They do not see themselves as aggressive or wishing to harm the child. On interview, many of them say they are afraid of the child and distort the size of the child, viewing the child as potentially dangerous. Some offenders are genuinely hurt when their aggressiveness is confronted. They view themselves as being unfairly treated and accused.

When their victims charge them with malicious intent, they feel wounded. Typical comments are: "How can Bobbie betray me? I loved him. I never touched him like that. I would never hurt him." For many pedophiles, such cognitive impairment (a concept from cognitive-behavioral theories) or denial is a critical part of their dysfunctional sexual patterns.

A familiar rationalization for the pedophilic act is: "I was just sexually educating him." Alternatively, the pedophile may claim that the child wanted it and asked for it. One 57-year-old man said, "I could tell by the way she approached me that she was interested in sex. Boys and girls who are seven enjoy sex and want sex." Often pedophiles see themselves, not the child, as the victims. These projections and cognitive distortions are typical of the lack of understanding and lack of empathy pedophiles have for children. Treatment programs must focus on these cognitive impairments.

The Ephebophile

The ephebophile's attraction to older children reflects a higher level of social and psychosexual development than does the pedophile's attraction to younger, prepubescent children. If the ephebophile chooses girls as victims, the attraction may be to their virginity and lack of sexual experience. Having sex with a virgin means not having to worry about how she compares you sexually to other men. If boys are victimized, the focus is on genital sex.

The sexual abuse of male teenagers by women is thought to be underreported owing to social and cultural forces. When an older woman coerces a teenage boy, it is unlikely that a report will be filed, although sexual exploitation has taken place. Society may look upon it as acceptable and call it an initiation of the boy into sexuality. In addition, if the teenage boy reports the molestation and it is publicized, he may become the target of ridicule and suffer more from the social ostracism than from the original abuse.

The ephebophile is often unaware that sexual coercion has taken place. He or she may say that the teen was not a victim and enjoyed both the sex act and the attention. A common argument by the perpetrator is that the teenager can choose to engage in sexual relationships. This argument not only denies social and legal standards, but also fails to appreciate the power of adult roles.

Adolescence is a time when issues of intimacy are highlighted and when idealism takes center stage. The teenager is vulnerable to subtle coercion by powerful adults who are viewed as role models and sometimes idealized, such as physicians, Scout leaders, and clergy. This is especially true when the clergy is involved. The clergy member uses the basic trust and spirituality of the youth as leverage to manipulate the adolescent into a sexual relationship.

One patient, a Catholic priest, molested a child and then adopted him. This converted the relationship into a pseudo-incestuous bond in which all parties were enmeshed in a destructive interaction. The illusion of a "loving family" was presented to the community.

Berlin reports that "having been sexually active with an adult during childhood, especially for a boy, increases the risk of developing an aberrant sexual appetite such as pedophilia" (Berlin & Coyle, 1981). The ephebophile who denies that any harm has been done or asserts that the adolescent freely chose to enter into the sexual relationship engages in a cognitive distortion and is demonstrating an impaired judgment, common attributes of both ephebophilia and pedophilia.

Common Characteristics
Pedophiles and ephebophiles differ in many respects but they share certain characteristics. Pither et al. (1988) summarize some of these universal elements:
- cognitive distortions
- deviant sexual fantasies
- disordered sexual arousal pattern
- interpersonal dependence

- low self-esteem
- low victim empathy
- planning of the sexual offense
- deficient sexual knowledge
- lack of social skills

The sexual offense is often precipitated by an inability to cope associated with increased stress, workaholism, alcohol abuse, profound feelings of loneliness and emptiness and a feeling of despair about their lack of connectedness to others. The sexual acting out results in a more pleasant emotional state (e.g., sexual excitement instead of depression) and provides the psyche with an internal experience of integration instead of disintegration.

Always an Aggressive Act
Pedophilia or ephebophilia is always an aggressive act. The perpetrator's lack of awareness of this aggressive component in the relationship is akin to disavowal or denial and is a delusional suspension of reality. Such persons may rationalize their molestation as serving a caretaker or parental role (taking the child/teen away for a holiday), performing an educational function (serving as a sex educator), or providing friendship (declaring that the child is "my best friend," even though there may be a 30-year age difference).

The establishment of an aggressive relationship gives the perpetrator, as has been suggested, power, control and dominance over the child and provides a connection to a real individual in order to overcome feelings of isolation and loneliness. During the "courtship" phase, the perpetrator disguises the aggression in order to manipulate the child and coerce him or her into participating in the "game" or "play."

The child's adoring or admiring attitude, or the teenager's idealization, is critical to the deception. This adoration and admiration feeds the narcissistic grandiosity of the perpetrators, provides them with a modicum of self-esteem, and confirms their self-image as loving and caring. Essentially, the victim unwittingly provides the pedophile/ephebophile with an important narcissistic balance to an otherwise depleted and depressed personality. The sexual encounter provides a feeling of cohesion to a psyche which is in danger of disintegrating.

Given the perpetrator's lack of self-assertion, psychosexual and psychosocial immaturity, and inability to form gratifying peer re-

lationships (especially heterosexual ones), the child/teenager is
an ideal object for sexual exploitation. Because the abuser lacks
genuine empathy and connectedness to others, the child or teenager is viewed as a pliable object that can be persuaded to relate
sexually to the adult.

Disturbed Thinking

During the sexual molestation, the aggressor's thinking is disturbed. Many sex offenders speak of the molestation as taking
place in a hypnotic-like trance from which they awaken only after
an orgasm. This trance is the mind's way of separating the rage
from consciousness. Some researchers might argue that this results from damage to the frontal and temporal lobes of their
brains, leading to poor judgment, blunted anxiety, and impulsivity. Moreover, the disappearance of sexually motivating fantasies
in the post-ejaculatory phase suggests a biological link between
the body's hormonal system and human cognition.

Overcoming a state of denial can be accomplished by a powerful intervention:

> *Mr. J., a 31-year-old exhibitionist, followed an 8-year-old girl from
> school as she took a shortcut through the woods. Overcome with a
> state of excitement, he felt flushed and thrilled at the idea of expos-
> ing himself and masturbating. Just as he closed in on her, another
> exhibitionist appeared and exposed himself to the girl. Mr. J. awoke
> from "my hypnotic-like state" and became incensed at the other
> man. "How could he do that to such an innocent girl?" he
> thought. Enraged, Mr. J. pursued the man with the intent of hav-
> ing him arrested.*

Only when another man interrupted Mr. J's reverie did he become morally outraged. This case highlights the split-off states of
consciousness that sex offenders may experience in order to disa-
vow the reality of their aggression.

A Game of Intimacy

In all cases, an attempt is made to engage the child/teenager in a
relationship. Khan (1979) has called this strategy a "technique of
intimacy" in which sexual excitement and altered ego states are
played out in games and scenarios that substitute an intense sexu-

al feeling for genuine intimacy. The true nature of the relationship is kept secret to maintain the fiction and to avoid confrontation. The "game of pretend" allows both parties to pretend that what is happening is not really happening.

The child, too, may be in a "dream-like" state induced by the aggressor. When the child awakens from the "trance" and recognizes the betrayal, there is a need to cleanse the self, to confess the "game," and to break the conspiracy of silence. The adults may feel victimized when a report is made and not understand why the child/teen has betrayed them. The destruction of the perpetrator's delusion that a genuine friendship has taken place may lead to a suicidal crisis.

Some pedophiles become increasingly aggressive and sadistic over time. The poem "Slayer of the Soul" gives testimony to how unresolved childhood traumas resurface during adulthood and are re-enacted so that the self can master the anxiety. In the poem, we see how John attempts to instill in the child, through projective identification (a psychological defense), his own disintegrated emotional state. Once the sexual fantasies are stimulated in the perpetrator, the addictive sexual cycle begins. Until it is broken, someone, somewhere, is at risk.

The Need for a Variety of Perspectives

Pedophilia and ephebophilia are heterogeneous disorders; no single perspective can explain them. We have established, however, that there are certain characteristics which these individuals have in common. A theory would have to explain why a particular content of the self is eroticized and how the aggressive and sexual issues are fused and confused. Psychoanalysis, and behavioral, social, and learning theories have all contributed to our understanding of why and how arousal patterns are established and how one's sexual drive becomes linked to a child or teenager. In most cases, it is the result of some early childhood experience in which patterns of behavior are firmly established. Familial studies (Lothstein, 1986) have provided evidence that unresolved, intergenerational conflicts wend their way into the sexual psychopathology of the individual and are acted out unmercifully.

Finally, the biological perspective allows us to see how our sexuality and aggression may be linked to organic factors that activate, if not organize, our sexuality. The fact that sexually deviant behavior is activated by stress and loneliness, and potentiated by alcohol, and perhaps brain pathology, suggests that paraphilic behavior may be an attempt to preserve the psychic integrity of someone who is floundering and moving toward a personality disintegration. In this sense, the inner experience of the sexual addiction may be viewed as evidence that self-cohesion has been lost and that the psyche is desperately trying to maintain itself as an intact, self-regulating system.

References

American Psychiatric Association. *Diagnostic and Statistical Manual of Mental Disorders, Revised (DSM III-R)*. Washington, D.C.: APA Press, 1987.

Araji, S. and Finkelhor, D. Explanations of pedophilia: Review of empirical research. *Bulletin of the American Academy of Psychiatry and Law*. 13: 17–37, 1985.

Barlow, D., and Wincze, J. Treatment of sexual deviations. In S.R. Leiblum and L. Peron (eds.) *Principles and Practice of Sex Therapy*. New York: Guilford Press, 1980.

Barnard, G., Fuller, A., Robbins, L., and Shaw, T. *The Child Molester: An Integrated Approach to Evaluation and Treatment*. New York: Brunner/Mazel, 1989.

Berlin, F. Issues on the exploration of biological factors contributing to the etiology of the "sex offender" plus some ethical considerations. In Prentky, R., & Quinsey, V. *Human Sexual Aggression: Current Perspectives*. Annals of the New York Academy of Science. 528: 183–192, 1988.

Berlin, F., and Coyle, G. Sexual deviation syndromes. *Johns Hopkins Medical Journal*. 149: 119–125, 1981.

Bradford, J., Bloomberg, D., and Bourget, D. The heterogeneity/homogeneity of pedophilia. *Psychiatry Journal University of Ottawa*. 13: 217–226, 1988.

Carnes, P. _Out Of The Shadows: Understanding Sexual Addiction._ Minneapolis: CompCare Publications, 1983.

Dube, R., and Martine, H. Sexual abuse of children under 12 years of age: A review of 511 cases. _Child Abuse & Neglect._ 12: 321–330, 1988.

Erickson, W., Walbek, N., and Seeley, R. Behavior patterns of child molesters. _Archives of Sexual Behavior._ 17: 77–86, 1988.

Fehlow, P. The female sexual delinquent. _Psychiatry, Neurology, and Medical Psychology (Leipz)._ 27: 612–618, 1975.

Finkelhor, D., and Lewis I. An epidemiologic approach to the study of child molestation. In Prentky, R., and Quinsey, V. _Human Sexual Aggression: Current Perspectives._ Annals of the New York Academy of Science. 528: 64–78, 1988.

Fuller, A. Child molestation and pedophilia: An overview for the physician. _Journal of the American Medical Association._ 261: 602–696, 1989.

Gaffney, G., and Berlin, F. Is there hypothalamic-pituitary-gonadal dysfunction in pedophilia? A pilot study. _British Journal of Psychiatry._ 145: 657–660, 1984.

Gaffney, G., Lurie, S., and Berlin, F. Is there familial transmission of pedophilia? Journal of Nervous and Mental Disease. 172: 546–548, 1984.

Groth, N., Hobson, W., and Gary, T. The child molester: Clinical observations. In J. Conte and D. Shore (eds.). _Social Work and Child Sexual Abuse._ New York: Haworth, 1982.

Hendricks, S., Fitzpatrick, D., Hartmann, K., Quaife, M., Stratbnucker, R., and Graber, B. Brain structure and function in sexual molesters of children and adolescents. _Journal of Clinical Psychiatry._ 49: 108–112, 1988

Khan, M. _Alienation in Perversions._ New York: International Universities Press, New York, 1979.

Lanyon, R. Theory and treatment in child molestation. *Journal of Consulting and Clinical Psychology.* 54: 176–182, 1986.

Litin, E., Giffin, M., and Johnson, A. Parental influence in unusual sexual behavior in children. *Psychoanalytic Quarterly.* 25: 37–55, 1956.

Lothstein, L. *Female-to-Male Transsexualism.* London: Routledge & Kegan Paul, 1983.

Lothstein, L. Development of gender self representation in gender disturbed children. *Tenth International Symposium on Gender Dysphoria.* Amsterdam: Academisch Ziekenhuss Virje Universiteit. June 9–12, 1987.

Lothstein, L., Cassens, G., and Ford, M. Electrical activity mapping and neuropsychological dysfunction in deviant sexual behavior. *The Journal of Neuropsychiatry and Clinical Neurosciences,* 1990.

Miller, B., Cummings, J., McIntyre, H., Ebers, G., and Grode, M. Hypersexuality or altered sexual preference following brain injury. *Journal of Neurology, Neurosurgery, and Psychiatry.* 49: 867–873, 1986.

Money, J. Paraphilias: phenomenology and classification. *American Journal of Psychotherapy.* 38: 164–179, 1984.

Newton, D. Homosexual behavior and child molestation: A review of the evidence. *Adolescence.* 13: 29–43, 1978.

Phillips, E.L. *The Social Skills Basis of Psychopathology.* New York: Grune & Stratton, 1978.

Pithers, W., Kashima, K., Cumming, G., Beal, L., and Buell, M. Relapse prevention and sexual aggression. In Prentky, R., and Quinsey, V. *Human Sexual Aggression: Current Perspectives.* Annals of the New York Academy of Science. 528: 244–260, 1988.

Rada, R. Alcoholism and the child molester. *Annals New York Academy of Science.* 273: 492–496, 1976.

Regenstein, Q., and Reich, P. Pedophilia occuring after the onset of cognitive impairment. *Journal of Nervous and Mental Disease.* 166: 794–798, 1978.

Scott, M., Cole, J., McKay, S., Olden, C., and Liggett, K. Neuropsychological performance of sexual assaulters and pedophiles. *Journal of Forensic Science.* 29: 1114–1118, 1984.

Socarides, C. *The Preoedipal Origin and Psychoanalytic Theory of Sexual Perversions.* New York: International Universities Press, 1988.

Stoller, R. *Perversion: The Erotic Form of Hatred.* New York: Pantheon, 1975.

The Treatment
of Child Sex Abusers in the Church

Frank Valcour, M.D.

There is some good news in the matter of treating those who sexually molest children within a church context. Pedophilia and ephebophilia, as well as other sexual behavior disorders, are quite treatable and successful treatment programs have flourished in church-affiliated institutions.

Traditionally, professional literature has contained relatively little on the treatment of aberrant sexual behavior and outcome studies have been rather pessimistic. It has also been widely accepted that individual, insight-oriented psychotherapy is not very effective in preventing the recurrence of problematic sexual behavior.

In recent years, however, the experience of several treatment centers does not warrant such therapeutic pessimism. In September 1989, one such treatment center, Saint Luke Institute, collated statistics on the 55 priest-child molesters who had completed its program. Most of these were in active follow-up programs and among this group there were no known relapses and no new allegations of improper behavior occurring after treatment. Of the 55, 32 were in some form of active ministry. The period of follow-up for some individuals was as long as four and a half years. Such success is remarkable. It is with enthusiasm and hope that the following comments on the treatment of pedophilia and ephebophilia in church personnel are offered.

It should be noted that the vast majority of the child molesters in church ministry, and hence in St. Luke's treatment program, are ephebophiles. Thus the population we serve is generally more psychologically intact and higher functioning than the average population of child molesters one might find in prison, for example.

Despite the positive results of treatment programs, one does not speak of cure. The paraphilias (sexual behavior disorders) are generally considered chronic, enduring conditions. Even a successfully treated pedophile remains aware of the allure of his or her sexual object preference. We do not fully understand what establishes sexual object preference nor do we know how to eradicate it.

John Money, Ph.D., provides persuasive evidence of the importance of biological factors, including prenatal hormonal influences (Money, 1988). On the other hand, Robert Stoller, M.D., another theorist of perversions, cites the specificity of some paraphilic behavior as necessarily rooted in an individual's unique developmental experience (Stoller, 1975). The genetic or hormonal interplay that could direct erotic interest to something as specific as, say, a navy blue, high-heeled shoe, is beyond the imagination of the even most fanatic biological determinist.

What seems to have allowed the more recent treatment successes is the view that sexually deviant behavior, though not curable, is treatable. Recovery from compulsive and harmful behavior and a program promoting physical, psychological and spiritual health is eminently possible. The treatment model is similar to the approach used in substance abuse. Even if the problematic behavior is intermittent and not experienced as an urgent craving, the child molester feels powerless over his or her sexual attraction toward youths. (This is an incredible burden from which most of us are spared.) Awareness and acceptance of this powerlessness is the door to a twelve-step recovery program that borrows heavily from the wisdom and practice of the fellowship of Alcoholics Anonymous. Undoubtedly, there are other ways of conceptualizing treatment. The success of this approach, however, warrants the attention given it in this chapter.

Risk Factors
Although no single etiology of pedophilia or ephebophilia is

known, the professional literature cites a variety of risk factors. These are conditions or experiences which appear to occur with greater frequency in those who develop sexual behavior problems in adult life. The experience of treatment centers generally confirms what is found in the technical literature.

These risk factors include:

1. Chromosomal abnormalities
2. Congenital disturbances
3. History of childhood trauma
 a. Physical/emotional abuse
 b. Emotional trauma at developmental periods
 c. Sexual abuse
4. Early and/or extensive sexual activity
5. Unusual repression of sexual awareness
6. Hormonal abnormalities
7. Neuro-psychological deficits.

It seems logical to begin a discussion of treatment by addressing risk factors even though some may not be dealt with in any substantive way until later phases of actual therapy. Some of these can be treated directly; others cannot be changed but acknowledging and explaining them can be helpful.

An example of an unalterable risk factor is the presence of a chromosomal abnormality. The most common of these is the sex chromosome aberration yielding what is called *Kleinfelter's Syndrome.* In this condition, the sex chromosome pattern is XXY. An individual with this chromosomal configuration is apt to have small genitals with undescended or atrophic testes, unusually long arms and perhaps some enlargement of breast tissue. Of close to a hundred child molesters known to this author, three are afflicted with this disorder and in two instances the condition was diagnosed as one of the reasons for sexual behavior problems. Knowing about this genetic condition provides some basis of reassurance to these individuals that their behavior has some origins beyond anyone's fault or control. Clarity about the nature of this risk factor can help them deal with it more realistically. Relatively simple cosmetic surgery can remove hypertrophied breast tissue, significantly improving one's body image.

Congenital conditions such as underdevelopment of genitals probably exert their effect on aberrant sexual behaviors in an indirect way. A distorted body image can easily lead to shyness and avoidance of the competition and exploration typical of normal development. In adolescence, the upsurge of sexual impulses and curiosity might be more comfortably exercised with younger, less developed and therefore less threatening acquaintances. This can set a pattern that may persist well into adult life. Addressing of body image concerns and their effect on relationships with peers is an appropriate psychotherapeutic goal.

Childhood Trauma

It is common for those being evaluated or treated for pedophilia or ephebophilia to give a developmental history featuring great emotional deprivation and/or significant abuse, be it physical, emotional or sexual. The deprivation may be occasioned by the early death of a parent, an unmanageably large family, divorce, or significant family illness.

The physical or emotional abuse found in a child molester's developmental background is probably not so different from that of other types of behaviorally disturbed persons. One pattern, however, is intriguing: it is not uncommon for child molesters to have gone through circumstances that, in effect, have robbed them of a portion of their childhood. Sometimes this occurs when one has had to take on a parent-like role, perhaps relating more like a partner to, rather than as a child of, the mate of an alcoholic spouse. Sometimes such situations are quite unusual, as when an early adolescent must provide daily nursing care to a gravely disabled older sibling. At times, the perpetrator's illicit sexual behavior seems to be an effort to give the emotional nurturance that he or she did not receive at the victim's age. When child abusers can admit their own human needs, acknowledge their legitimacy, and address them appropriately, the risk of stereotypic, compulsive acting-out is reduced.

History of Abuse

A history of being abused sexually presents both problems and opportunities in treatment. "Do unto others as you have been done to" is a resilient rule of personality development. In clinical work with pedophilic or ephebophilic priests and religious, somewhere between a third and a half give a history of childhood sexual mistreatment. Not uncommonly, such abuse was at the hands of a priest. Relatives, family friends and significantly older (four years or more) neighborhood children are also common perpetrators. Sexual abuse by anonymous adults happens, but is less often found in this treatment population.

A history of abuse can be a problem if the abuser is a friendly and nurturing figure. These circumstances may make it difficult for individuals in treatment to identify how they were harmed by the experience. This, in turn, supports their own denial in owning up to the harm they have done. Taken in another direction, their anger and sense of violation can be felt as both explanation and justification for their own abuse of children.

It can happen in treatment that an individual will gain access to a repressed memory of sexual abuse. A similar phenomenon occurs when a recollection of ambiguous behavior becomes clarified as actually constituting sexual abuse. Typically, such treatment experiences greatly enhance perspective on the meaning of one's own behavior. For the most part, priests and religious in treatment are not amoral. In fact, the tendency is for them to be hyper-moralistic. When the denial and cognitive distortions around their sexual behavior are corrected, their commitment to avoid such behavior is usually very deep.

It has been our clinical experience that a variety of victimizations have occurred in the developmental history of child molesters. Even in the absence of a clear background of being abused, they tend to perceive themselves as victims of the church, the media, and/or the courts. Even treatment is often felt as another trial and imposition. It is a major task to help the individuals admit and heal their own history of being abused through grief and forgiveness work. It is only then that they are able to surrender the oft-assumed role of victim.

Contributing Factors

Early Experiences Timing is a critical facet of the unfolding of life, both biologically and socially. There are experimental data to suggest that the level of androgens (male sex hormones) at critical moments of fetal life affect later behaviors associated with sexual orientation. In human growth and development, sexual awareness, curiosity, and experimentation fall within a loosely defined normative range. Problems with the integration of one's sexuality tend to occur when there is early or excessive sexual stimulation or activity, or when there is delayed or inordinately repressed sexual experience. The former circumstances tend to promote sexual preoccupation and an eroticization of all relational contact. The latter tend to drop the individual into adulthood with poorly formed and ineffective mechanisms of discrimination and control. The correction in therapy of these developmental disturbances can be quite difficult. Education, behavioral coaching, and disclosure among peers all have a role.

Hormonal Problems   The sexual drive can be thought of as having both direction and intensity. In essence, the whole problem of pedophilia/ephebophilia involves a deflection of the normal direction of sexual interest. The intensity of the drive can aggravate the problem of coping with the direction. Blood levels of testosterone have some relationship to this intensity. The use of antiandrogen medication is valuable in reducing elevated testosterone levels. This will be discussed more extensively below. Subtler hormonal abnormalities are often more difficult to correct. Knowing about them and their association with behavioral problems can help alleviate some destructive, self-condemning tendencies in patients.

Neuropsychological Deficits   Neuropsychology is that field of study that examines brain-behavior relationships. The human brain is the mediator both of behavior and subjective experience. The clinical population of priest child molesters exhibits an unusually high incidence of measurable abnormalities in specific brain functions. Sometimes these deficits are minor, at other times more significant. In the latter instance, they may be of such magnitude that the abstract thinking capacity necessary to reflect on one's own behavior, learn what occasions it, and make suitable plans to compensate is simply not there. In such a case, supervision and a protective environment, but not treatment, are the appropriate response. In less severe situations, compensatory strategies may be helpful.

   In the successful treatment of pedophiles and ephebophiles, two clinical phenomena must be aggressively addressed and their status continually monitored throughout treatment. These are *denial* and *countertransference.*

Denial   Denial might be defined as the inability to acknowledge the facts of one's experience and behavior and/or the emotional significance of those facts. Denial in and of itself is not pathological. It is part of ordinary human experience and is one of several "mechanisms of defense." These mechanisms keep disruptive, threatening, or otherwise unacceptable perceptions out of our awareness. Mechanisms of defense, including denial, are necessary for day-to-day human functioning. Perhaps a universal experience of denial is the way we function in an emergency situation, only admitting into awareness the terror of the threat of imminent death after that threat has been avoided. Another common example is the disbelief one often has when hearing of the death of a loved one or the diagnosis of a fatal illness. When the individual is prepared to cope, the initial disbelief (denial) fades. This mechanism of defense helps to preserve the emotional stability necessary for on-going daily function.

In some situations, what is meant to protect the individual actually becomes destructive. This is very characteristic of addictions. The alcoholic is often the last to recognize how much trouble alcohol is causing in his or her life. Some element of denial is almost always found in sexual behavior disorders, especially in those who sexually abuse children.

The essence of the child molester's denial is a belief that the acts or predilection to them are not primarily sexual. On superficial examination, this seems absurd. How can a 40-year-old adult fondle the genitals of a 15-year-old youth and not believe he is engaged in a sexual act? An understanding of this denial can begin with a little reflection on what is at stake emotionally and psychologically.

Suppose Father X enters the minor seminary at age 15 and until ordination at age 26 has virtually no support in examining and accepting ordinary human sexual impulses. After 15 years of a workaholic lifestyle, he says the funeral mass for his deceased mother, who had been the major emotional affirmer of his religious vocation. (One-third of his seminary class has left the priesthood.) He has been a shy person who finds it easier to relate to adolescents, particularly those hungry for non-abusive and sympathetic adult attention. Pastors and parishioners have appreciated his devotion to an age group that many find spoiled, irresponsible, and unpleasant. On an overnight trip with a group of teenagers, accommodations are cramped and beds are shared to cut expenses. In grief, fatigue, and loneliness during the night Father X embraces the youth beside him and eventually fondles him. Upon arising the next day, a kind of terror starts to surface within as the threat to his career, reputation, life of commitment and priesthood becomes palpable. One way to avoid this intolerable danger is for the felonious act to be seen as something other than it was, something benign, maybe even praiseworthy. "Maybe it wasn't sexual." "Maybe it was just a need for comforting."

This type of cognitive distortion is probably the most common form of denial we see in priest and religious child molesters. "It wasn't lust; it was affection." The denial of sexual interest and gratification is typically shored up by rationalization. This is an alternative explanation of the behavior that helps the individual to swallow his or her own distortion.

Other rationalizations also deny any erotic intent:

"It was playfulness, wrestling, or horsing around."

"It was educational. He was very concerned about his genital size and I was examining him to reassure him that he was normal."

"It was for health purposes. He complained of back pain and I was giving him a complete massage to relax him."

There are more complicated rationalizations which often are based on dimly perceived assumptions. "Sexual acts with boys are not really as sexual as they would be with girls." "He came on to me so the motivation was really his." One might ask how denial can be distinguished from outright lying. The answer is twofold: sometimes it cannot and sometimes the distinction may not make much difference.

Therapy begins with an assault on denial/lying. Individuals must be brought to an awareness that their behavior with youth has been sexual and has been actually or potentially grievously harmful. The first blow against the fortress of denial is usually the religious superior's intervention. Being told that others, victims or their families, have found the priest's or religious' behavior to be damaging may be the first time that the individual has had to entertain consciously that reality. For a few, the intervention may be experienced as a relief. Such individuals have already experienced erosion of their denial and started to feel the conflict between legitimate human needs and an illegitimate pattern of coping with them.

The availability of peer pressure and peer support seems to be indispensable in working with denial. Perpetrators of child sexual abuse can recognize in each other all the subterfuges and evasions which say "it isn't so." There is also the element of identification and support. *The freedom to talk to another human being about something never shared in one's entire life can be a remarkable step on a healing journey.*

One refinement of the peer pressure/peer support situation is the delivery of a "behavior log." In this technique, individuals present to a group of fellow patients the development of their sexual behavior problem from its earliest discernable beginning to the present. To be useful, this narration must be fully disclosing, long on description, and short on explanation. The listening patients can then offer to the sharers their observations on their perceived truthfulness, depth of acknowledgment of the behavior problem, areas of ambiguity, and so forth. If one tries to call to mind the most shameful elements of one's past and pictures the humble sharing of this brokenness with peers, then one begins to get a grasp on the intensity and power of this therapeutic device.

A certain amount of denial can be removed by education. Knowledge of normal sexual development is often dramatically lacking in child molesters. At a more confrontive level, studies of the harmfulness of sexual abuse can be utilized to help individuals grasp why their behavior is felonious. At the most confrontive level, the reading of victim impact statements is potentially useful in blasting through denial. These are not always available, especially if criminal charges or civil litigation has not gone forward.

How does one know that progress has been made in undermining denial? This is a matter of clinical judgment with criteria of widely varying reliability. If an individual shares information with his therapist or treatment team that has not been obtained from other sources, it is an excellent sign that denial has been substantially neutralized. An ability to recognize and explain a ritual or pattern of behavior that builds up to an improper act, together with a willingness to take action to break the pattern, is another good sign. A heartfelt commitment to do whatever is necessary not to hurt any more children is a desired outcome of treatment. The recognition of "heartfelt commitment" is not easy and, at this point, seems to depend on a blend of extensive clinical experience and the evidence of a variety of compassionate and humane behaviors.

Countertransference   Countertransference is a technical term with various interpretations. For the purposes of this chapter, it will be defined as the emotional responses evoked *in the therapist* by the patient in treatment, particularly those responses to the patient's problems or pathology. Those attempting to treat child molesters have to admit consciously that their patients have frequently committed heinous acts. In the eyes of society, including a prison society, these individuals are among the "lowest of the low." The loathing of society is often part of the patient's self-image but this is usually at a repressed level, particularly early in treatment.

Most therapists, being moral people and law-abiding citizens, are inclined to react to child molesters as does the bulk of society—with revulsion and horror. Denial of these reactions can disqualify a therapist from doing meaningful work with such patients. Acceptance of these feelings, however, does not mean they are dealt with. A working knowledge of risk factors and an effort to understand the development of this individual's perversion are necessary for therapists to overcome their prejudicial attitudes. As experience is acquired, the therapist will, it is hoped, move to a balanced perspective. He or she will come to see that the criminal behavior, as odious as it may be, cannot be taken as the total measure of this person's worth. Acceptance of a person does not equal acceptance of his or her deeds.

A less obvious countertransference reaction is the ignoring or minimizing of the harmfulness of the perverse behavior. It is natural for a therapist to side with patients, to take their part, and to try to be helpful. As mentioned before, many perpetrators were themselves victims of sexual abuse. Most tend to see themselves as having been victimized, either sexually or otherwise. Therapists, in their zeal to be supportive, can be seduced into allying with the "victim" side of the patient. This can be a serious interference with the confrontive, "tough love" stance that is often necessary in working through the patient's denial. The issues of denial and countertransference intertwine throughout treatment. They are *never* fully resolved. What is needed is a recognition of their durability and a continual willingness to review and reassess their influence.

Psychotherapeutic Work

A discussion of denial and countertransference leads to a broader review of the psychotherapeutic work with this patient population. In the past, individual, insight-oriented psychotherapy has been considered rather ineffective in preventing the recurrence of sexual behavior problems. The result was not unlike attempts to treat alcoholics or other substance abusers by individual therapy alone. The theoretical approach was logical. "If you find out why they do these things and change them, then the undesired behavior should stop." Logic did not carry the day.

The 12-Step Approach

With alcoholism, the beginning of Alcoholics Anonymous over 50 years ago provided a new approach that worked. The drinking itself was the problem, not the thousands of reasons people gave to explain why they drank. The AA philosophy and decades of accumulated wisdom support what is called a 12-step approach to recovery. (See appendix.) The 12 steps involve a spirituality that occasions conversion and renewal in those who can embrace it. Critical aspects of the 12-step recovery model have been adapted to the treatment programs for the sexual behavior disorders.

There is clinical controversy over the concept of "sexual addiction." It is not yet an official psychiatric term but some treatment centers are quite effective in their utilization of an "addictive model." Utilization of 12-step concepts does not require either the subjective admission of the term "sexual addict" or resolution of the theoretical question of whether or not sexual addiction truly exists.

Inasmuch as we do not choose our sexual orientation, we are powerless over that aspect of our experience. That is not to say we have no responsibility for our behavior. For the pedophile, the sexual appeal of a prepubescent child is not something that can be wished away. Acceptance of this fact can lead to a profound awareness of and hope for help from outside oneself (a higher power). The third step in the AA framework is the handing over of self to that healing higher power, be it God, a fellowship or therapy group, a treatment center, or some combination thereof.

This acceptance of a problem, awareness of help, and handing of one's self over to a healing process is never total. Once it begins it opens a person to psychotherapy which, it is hoped, works in concert with the 12-step model.

Common Therapeutic Problems

The psychotherapeutic work with child molesters entails almost every dimension of human life, but the more common aspects of such treatment include:

- idealization of family, religious life, self
- authority conflicts
- control issues
- self-loathing
- need for forgiveness.

Idealization Despite the tendency of perpetrators to see themselves as victims, they often idealize their families or developmental backgrounds. The idealization often takes the form of minimizing the impact of adverse circumstances. (One fellow who moved about 20 times before graduating from high school said this was not much of a problem because the family had a comfortable house.) It may take the form of affirming the motivation of those who did not handle their responsibilities well. ("Yes, my father often drank too much but we always knew that he loved us.") Families vary greatly in their capacity to tolerate pain and conflict. Sometimes pain and the unmet needs which occasion it are simply not acknowledged. For such idealizations, psychotherapy does not aim at blaming or excusing but more at helping a person more fully accept the reality of personal history, making some sense out of his or her manner of adapting and coping.

For those who can face childhood trauma, treatment may involve gaining perspective on it, acknowledging lingering resentments, and offering forgiveness. In cases where offenders themselves had been sexually abused as children, the recovery, exploration, and resolution of that pain can be very important in freeing them to work with their own problematic behavior.

Authority Conflicts The vast majority of priest and religious child abusers become involved with adolescents. There are some emerging data that their own psychosexual development may be arrested at the adolescent level. Consistent with this thesis, many have significant authority conflicts. They may vigorously desire the attention, approval and affection of their bishops while at the same time feel that the bishops are over-controlling and oppressive. In a treatment center as well, one commonly sees these types of authority conflicts. For example, the therapy staff is denigrated and disparaged, yet their absence due to vacation or sickness is greeted with anger or regressive fearfulness. What is missing is a mature view of authority as a fact of life in any social structure. It must be dealt with through honest communication and mutual recognition of roles and responsibilities.

Control Issues   Related to authority conflicts is preoccupation with control. A fragile sense of self, distrust of authority, and experiences of being hurt can easily lead to believing that trusting others is too hazardous. Spontaneous interaction in relationships is replaced by strict role-related behavior or routines of manipulation. In a therapeutic community setting, such preoccupation with control can be brought to awareness. The behaviors manifesting it can be described and alternative behaviors suggested and explored.

Self-loathing   Early in treatment, a patient may try to impress both staff and fellow patients. The following behaviors are often observed: being of service, entertaining others, or dis-identifying with the group ("It's a mistake that I'm here"). Through disclosure in psychotherapy the individual might face profound feelings of self-loathing and guilt. A happy outcome occurs when individuals can despise their offensive behavior yet still experience themselves as fully franchised human beings loved by God and others.

Need for Forgiveness   The effective erosion of denial will, it is hoped, bring the perpetrator into full confrontation with the harm he or she has done to others. In the case of priests, this harm extends beyond the individual victim to include the priest's family, his superiors, his parish or other ministry, and the church at large. It is a good sign when the individual can admit to having harmed, at least potentially, those who have not complained or brought charges. This admission naturally leads to a search for forgiveness, and where possible, to the making of amends. One indicator of this type of progress in therapy is the calm, albeit painful, acceptance of the negative consequences of one's behavior.

Additional Areas of Treatment
In addition to the therapy directed at the sexual behavior problems themselves or issues intimately associated with them, there is a need to address both coexisting conditions and aspects of balanced emotional health that may be grossly underdeveloped. Many pedophiles and ephebophiles have more than one psychiatric diagnosis. They may be afflicted with substance abuse, eating

problems or depression as well as their sexual disorder. There is a need for careful clinical judgment here. The other diagnoses must be treated if the recovering patient is to experience some sense of health and joy in life. On the other hand, perspective and priorities can quickly be obscured if the child molester thinks he or she is in treatment because of compulsive overeating.

The matter of substance abuse has particular relevance because of the disinhibiting effects on behavior of alcohol and other drugs. A sober lifestyle is critical for the alcoholic pedophile/ephebophile, yet it is a dangerous simplification to think that alcoholism is the cause of one's sexual aberration. It is obvious that not all alcoholics have sexual behavior problems.

The self-loathing mentioned above may be the emotional underpinning of self-neglect that eventually becomes habitual. Eating, grooming and suitable levels of exercise are often ordinary human activities that the perpetrator manages poorly. The closeness of life in a therapeutic community often highlights one's neglect of these ordinary practices of daily living.

At a more complex level of organization are recreational habits. Extended or individual contact with youth is off-limits for the recovering pedophile or ephebophile. For many of them, their leisure and entertainment was with adolescents. If new activities are not developed, major emotional deprivation will be a feature of recovery and will eventually corrode it.

A substantial amount of reparative work often is needed for underdeveloped aspects of the perpetrator's personality. The black or white, all or nothing, mentality typical of some phases of adolescence must be transcended. Interpersonal hesitancy and shyness can be helped with assertiveness training.

All of us probably have our limits when it comes to relationships and closeness to one another. The studious, reclusive person is unlikely to become the gregarious social butterfly. Part of maturation involves some experimentation and self-assessment to find our own healthy level of intimacy and human connectedness. This maturation should be based on a recognition of the legitimacy of our human need for affection. Treatment will involve an opportunity to practice relationship-building skills. The quality of peer relationships is characteristically low in child molesters. An increase in self-esteem helps set the stage for coaching and practice in forming friendships.

Depo-Provera

In years past, stubborn rates of recidivism among sexual offenders led to trials of drastic treatment methods. Some foreign studies of repeat offenders attested to partial success with castration. This method of treatment, however, has not been used to any great extent in the United States or Canada.

Since the mid-1970s, though, a reversible form of "chemical castration" has been available by using anti-androgenic medication. Early studies on a criminal population revealed remarkable results in preventing the recurrence of felonious behavior in the experimental group. Success in preventing relapse was well into the ninetieth percentile. Persuasive arguments can be made that in personality structure, life course, and clinical history, priests and religious child molesters differ from the population studied in the original research on this use of anti-androgenic medication. For example, the majority of priests and religious treated in the United States have not passed through the criminal justice system. Nonetheless, the dramatic value of this treatment in the original studies almost forces consideration of its use in the treatment of priests and religious.

The most common anti-androgenic drug used for suppressing sexual drive and appetite is injectable Medroxy-progesterone acetate (depo-provera). Orally administered M.P.A. works less reliably and has more side effects. Cyproterone acetate (Androcur) has been used with positive results but is not currently available in the United States.

Depo-provera is an FDA-approved drug that is used in the treatment of certain female cancers. It also has some contraceptive applications. In men, it has been found to lower sharply serum testosterone levels. Several mechanisms appear to account for this effect, including the induction of enzymes involved in metabolizing testosterone and the turning off of a hormonal signal from the pituitary gland to the testes. It may also have some central effects, that is, direct effects on the brain itself. This is merely speculative, however; on a clinical basis, a non-specific, emotional calming effect is inconsistently observed.

What is more reliably observed is a marked decrease in sexual interest, sexual response and, most important, sexual behavior. Those on the drug usually report a decrease in erotic imagery in dreams, less physical arousal, and a comforting sense of manageability of sexual urges. For many, these effects are described as a

sense of freedom. It is as if a burden of many years duration has
been lifted.

Sometimes a paradoxical effect is observed, that is, a person reports a clearer awareness of what types of persons are found to be
of sexual interest. Before taking the drug, such individuals had
controlled their behavior through almost a total repression of sexual interest and awareness. Once the pressure to engage in inappropriate acts is reduced to a non-threatening level, the person
can admit into consciousness the fantasies and perceptions that
used to be too dangerous. This sense of safety permits a therapeutic exploration of this dimension of one's self and can lead to a
more mature sense of understanding and integration.

Depo-provera is a clinically interesting drug. Though very useful as part of an overall treatment program, it is not a panacea.
Like any drug, it tends to work best when its beneficial effect is
understood and desired by the individual taking it. A discussion
with a patient in treatment about possible use of depo-provera is
often informative. When denial has been largely dealt with, a patient is usually ready to try whatever is recommended if it will
help to prevent further acting out. Such an individual approaches
a talk about depo-provera with an interest in how it may be helpful and with relatively little concern about the inconvenience of
the drug and its possible side effects.

Those who have not fully accepted the nature and extent of
their illness try to marshall arguments against this drug. They refer to it as "experimental," they become preoccupied with certain
side effects, and they request a second opinion. Certainly anyone
considering a medical treatment has a right to a second opinion.
Resistant individuals, however, tend to seek advice from physicians not familiar with the use of depo-provera and usually not
very knowledgeable about the treatment of sexual behavior disorders.

Depo-provera, however, does have risks and side effects that
must be explained to a patient for whom it is recommended.
Among its serious effects can be an increase in blood pressure, an
elevation of blood sugar, and the possibility of an increase in the
incidence of phlebitis (inflammation of veins). If any of these conditions are already present, the benefit of using the drug has to be
carefully weighed against the risk of aggravating these conditions. Each case is different and there is no easy formula to assist
in making such a tough decision. It is important to remember

what is at stake here. Society takes child abuse very seriously. These acts are usually considered felonies and, when tried, can lead to significant prison terms. At times, one may seem justified in asking what right an individual has to refuse something so obviously protective of the public.

Less serious side effects are weight gain, cold intolerance, intermittent feelings of fatigue and night sweats. Doses in the 200 to 300 mg. range given weekly by injection usually produce little in the way of troublesome side effects. Monitoring of the drug's use is done with a combination of laboratory tests and clinical assessment. After a person has been taking the drug for several months, the dosage interval can often be stretched out to two or three weeks with little loss of therapeutic effect. There is little effect on secondary sex characteristics, no loss of facial hair, raising of the voice or general change in pattern of interests. (The author is aware of the loss of body hair in two older gentlemen, which appears to have been an acceleration of a normal aging phenomenon.)

The question of how long an individual should take depo-provera is not easily answered. It appears most useful for those near the two ends of a clinical continuum. First are those at the healthy end who understand their illness, are committed to sexual sobriety, and will do anything not to act out. Second are those who minimize their problem, try to do as little as they can to promote recovery, and see *treatment* as their problem rather than the illegal behavior that brought them to it. For the former, depo-provera is a useful tool. For the latter, it may be the only thing standing between them and acting out.

As a person grows in sobriety, the relative importance of the various elements in the recovery program changes. For some, after two, three or more years of sexual abstinence, depo-provera may have a minor role. If its role does not justify the risks of taking it, it should be stopped. A sign of healthy sobriety is the willingness of the individual to negotiate openly and honestly this change with the prescribing physician. Unilateral decisions or strong pressure on the physician to alter the dose or discontinue the drug should always be viewed with suspicion.

Aftercare
Consistent with the view that pedophilia and ephebophilia are treatable but incurable conditions, an aftercare program is essential. Aftercare should not only maintain the gains made in

treatment, but should expand and extend the benefits of recovery to more and more aspects of a patient's life. The lore of Alcoholics Anonymous describes a pattern of recovery. The first year a person gets well physically, the second year emotionally and the third year spiritually.

For the person embracing a twelve-step recovery plan for deviant sexual behavior involving young people, there is usually little damage to physical health. What we think we are seeing is a somewhat delayed and less dramatic development of a sense of well-being. A person may not feel truly well until the second or third year of sexual sobriety. In any case, it is clear that ongoing efforts are necessary both to guard against relapse and to promote psychological, emotional and spiritual health.

Individuals should leave the initial phase of treatment with a clearly articulated and readily understood plan. This may be in the form of a contract or other written document that can be shared with others. In essence, it is a statement by individuals of how they intend to manage their sexual behavior disorder. It should include the description of specific behaviors. The performance of these can be recognized both by the individual and by external observers.

These external observers might be friends, relatives, religious superiors, or spiritual advisers. When they are asked to support the individual in following an aftercare plan, they become part of an external structure of accountability. If an individual has profited significantly from treatment, he or she will understand the need for external accountability. The person in recovery will not view that structure as oppressive or controlling but as concerned and supportive.

A deep understanding of one's paraphilia typically includes those circumstances and behaviors which put a person at risk for acting out. Sometimes these indicators of a weakening program are called "budding signs." Discussing one's "budding signs" with a support group permits the interruption of a regressive trend before the really problematic behavior recurs. When a defined program of recovery is being followed, the risk of relapse becomes minimal.

Results and Prognosis

Generally speaking, the results of treatment of priests and religious who have sexually abused children are excellent. At one facility, The Saint Luke Institute, 55 child molesters had completed treatment by September 1989. Of those in active follow-up (most of them), there were no reported instances of relapse and no new allegations of child molestation. Even allowing for the possibility of some improper behavior that was not brought to light, these are remarkable statistics. *Pessimism about the effectiveness of treatment is simply not warranted.* But these numbers should not be misinterpreted. Some of the individuals, though sexually abstinent, are quite impaired. Sometimes risk factors or personality deficits are so intractable that those in recovery have little to offer others once their basic ongoing recovery needs have been met. For the majority, however, the admission and treatment of their illness has led to a new level of psychological and spiritual health.

Can the recovering perpetrator of child abuse ever minister again? Well, approximately 32 of the 55 mentioned above are productively engaged in some form of ministry. It is usual to have some strictures imposed which honor public sensibilities as well as to help the individual steer clear of risk situations. Of those who are not in ministry, their inactive state is usually not of their own choosing.

The decision regarding reassignment for a treated priest or religious child molester is both weighty and complicated. In the face of this burden, some religious superiors have opted for the advice proffered by the legalists: "Take no risk." This extreme position fails to recognize that no decision is without risk.

To offer even a limited ministry assignment in a responsible way, a bishop or superior needs to obtain from a treating facility a formal opinion regarding the potential for relapse. Although this opinion can never be a guarantee, its reliability is enhanced to the degree the following factors are present:

1. Acknowledgment and acceptance of the nature and extent of one's condition manifested by a capacity to describe it to a superior in simple terms.

2. A commitment from the recovering person to do whatever is necessary to prevent the recurrence of problematic behavior. This typically includes abiding by recommendations of the treating facility regarding patient counseling, living arrangements, etc. Such a commitment is best put in written form, referring to specific forms of behavior. Inasmuch as the commitment is demonstrated by behavior, it can be monitored by others.

3. An awareness of one's own risk factors so thorough that the person in recovery can list and describe these factors to another person. Obviously an assignment would need to exclude working with individuals or in situations which would put others or the recovering person at risk.

4. A willingness on the part of the recovering individual to disclose fully to a small group of individuals the nature and extent of his or her problem so that he or she might ask for support and behavioral monitoring. This small group might include a pastor, spiritual director, family member or personnel director.

5. A participation in the formal aftercare program of the treating facility.

It is recommended that a diocese or religious community develop and promulgate a personnel policy which spells out conditions for reassignment. It should include reference to the factors above as well as some specifics about how accountability is to be measured. Scheduled meetings with a personnel director, release of information to superiors, and inclusion of a superior's delegate in a support group are some of the mechanisms to insure accountability. Such a policy, publicly stated and stringently followed, would establish a "customary standard of practice." It is hard to see how a superior following a customary standard of practice could be faulted for negligence.

As the awareness of treatment success for sexual behavior problems grows, individual priests and religious are beginning to request evaluation and/or treatment themselves. This is a profoundly hopeful development. If a bishop or superior indiscriminately suspends all who have committed child sexual abuse, this process will be stopped. A priest will not ask for treatment if it automatically means resigning from the priesthood.

At a philosophical level, compassion, forgiveness, and healing have always been central to the spirit and mission of the church. Persons who have truly come to terms with a sexual behavior disorder have much to say and much to witness regarding the authenticity of the paschal mystery. Their journey from a life of falsity through a valley of self-reproach and abject humiliation to a new life made possible by forgiveness, gives them personal resources that should not be ignored. Not the least of these resources is the possibility of speaking a message of hope to those with similar afflictions.

The church has often been criticized for what some see as

insensitive and unrealistic positions on sexual issues. In the matter of pedophilia and ephebophilia, this author thinks the church has taken a responsive and aggressive role. The old tactics of removal and concealment have been all but abandoned. Enlightened pastoral approaches to both victims and perpetrators have become the norm. In recognizing and supporting the successfully treated priest or religious through appropriate reassignment, the church has an opportunity to continue to give prophetic witness.

Appendix
The 12 Steps of Sexaholics Anonymous

1. We admitted that we were powerless over lust—that our lives had become unmanageable.

2. Came to believe that a Power greater than ourselves could restore us to sanity.

3. Made a decision to turn our will and our lives over to the care of God *as we understood Him.*

4. Made a searching and fearless moral inventory of ourselves.

5. Admitted to God, to ourselves and to another human being the exact nature of our wrongs.

6. Were entirely ready to have God remove all these defects of character.

7. Humbly asked Him to remove our shortcomings.

8. Made a list of all persons we had harmed, and became willing to make amends to them all.

9. Made direct amends to such people wherever possible, except when to do so would injure them or others.

10. Continued to take personal inventory and when we were wrong promptly admitted it.

11. Sought through prayer and meditation to improve our conscious contact with God *as we understood Him,* praying only for knowledge of His will for us and the power to carry that out.

12. Having had a spiritual awakening as the result of these Steps, we tried to carry this message to sexaholics, and to practice these principles in all our affairs.

References

Money, John, Ph.D. *Love Maps: Clinical Concepts of Sexual/Erotic Health and Pathology, Paraphilia, and Gender Transposition in Childhood, Adolescence, and Maturity.* New York: Prometheus Books, 1988.

Stoller, Robert J., M.D. *Perversion: The Erotic Form of Hatred.* Washington, D.C.: American Psychiatric Press, Inc., 1975.

Children as Victims of Sexual Abuse

Patricia A. Moran, ACSW, LICSW

Occurrence of Abuse

Knowledge of sexual abuse, aside from personal experience, comes from two primary sources: popular recountings and professional studies. In the past several years, there has been an increase of coverage of sexual abuse in newspapers, television, and other media. While such exposure heightens awareness of this problem, the facts are not easy to accept. It is not pleasant to think of a 4-year-old girl forced to perform oral sex with her uncle. To protect ourselves from this horror, it is all too easy to imagine that if sexual abuse does occur, it happens in another city, in a different social class, or to individuals who are, somehow, not like us. *None of this is true. Sexual abuse happens in our towns, in our parishes, and even in our own families.*

J. Herman (1981) gives a comprehensive overview of the history of therapists dealing with the issues of sexual abuse, beginning with Sigmund Freud. In 1896, Freud wrote that the origins of hysteria were childhood sexual abuses. His own discomfort with implicating "respectable" men led him to repudiate his theory less than one year later and he would then attribute hysteria to an unsuccessful resolution of Oedipal fantasies. His impact on the field resounded for many years, during which there was little mention of child sexual abuse. Herman tells us that it was only a half-century after Freud that incest was "rediscovered."

Prior to 1960, there were only four studies done on the prevalence of sexual abuse, including the famous Kinsey Report. In the last decade, there have been more than fifteen such studies indicating the resurgence of professional interest in this problem (Finkelhor, 1986).

Research studies that attempt to document the occurrence of sexual abuse can be of two types: *incidence studies*, which estimate the number of new cases in a given period of time, and *prevalence studies*, which research the percentage of abuse in the general population (Finkelhor, 1986). Because there are logistical problems with both types of studies, neither is an exact measurement. Robinson (1989) points out barriers to determining the true rates of sexual abuse: the highly taboo nature of the subject, the disturbing quality of the material, conflicting views of which population to sample (victims or offenders), and how exactly to define sexual abuse. The numbers and percentages resulting from studies reflect a wide range of statistics, some of which do not always agree. However, what we *do* know from studies and experience is that there has been a massive increase in the number of reported cases. A look at some of the research can provide a context from which to view the problem of child sexual abuse.

Incidence studies are based on surveying professionals who deal with these cases. One of the largest of these studies was commissioned by the National Center on Child Abuse and Neglect (NCCAN). Entitled "Study of National Incidence and Prevalence," it was published in 1980. In this study, it was estimated that 44,700 cases of child sexual abuse were known to professionals in 1979. The follow-up study in 1988 reports that the number of such cases had more than tripled. This dramatic increase was attributed to professionals being better attuned to the signs of abuse rather than to an actual increase in the number of incidents. This NCCAN study estimated that 45,000 to 200,000 new cases of child sexual abuse occur each year. If this were a medical disease, it would be an epidemic!

The prevalence studies are based on adults reporting on their childhood experiences. Kinsey (1953) reported that 24 percent of females had preadolescent sexual contact with an older male. Finkelhor, in his sampling of college students (1979), reported 19 percent of females and 9 percent of males had sexual experiences as children with an older partner, and 15 percent of females and 6 percent of males in his random sample in the Boston area had similar experiences (1984).

One of the largest research studies (Russell, 1986) shows an even greater occurrence. In a random sample of 930 women in the San Francisco area, 38 percent had an unwanted sexual experience involving physical contact prior to the age of 18. When Russell's definition of abuse was broadened to include non-contact sexual experience, such as exhibitionism and voyeurism, the numbers increased to 54 percent.

The definition of child sexual abuse varies in different studies with respect to the age limits of those included in the study, the type of behavior defined as abuse, and the defining characteristics of abuse (Finkelhor, 1986). This chapter will define child sexual abuse as any unwanted sexual advance on a child under the age of 18 by a person who is at least five years older.

A Profile of Victims

Research and experience indicate that the victims are both male and female. Finkelhor (1986) reviewed eight random sample community surveys and calculated that 71 percent of the victims are females and 29 percent are males. Although it is generally believed that the number of males is underreported, there is enough indication to state that girls are generally at higher risk of being abused.

The age range of child victims is from infancy to eighteen years old. Although the abuse may not necessarily cease then, it is no longer called child abuse. Finkelhor (1979) found the mean age at the time of onset of the abuse to be 10.6 years old in boys and girls. Herman (1981) found the mean age of 9.4 at the time of onset for girls. Russell (1986) reports the mean age of 10.62 for victims who reported extreme trauma. The variation in these numbers is not statistically significant; the constant is that preadolescent children are at the highest risk for being sexually abused.

Contrary to the myth of a man hiding in a dark alley or lurking behind the bushes in a trench coat, *most children are sexually abused by someone they know and trust.* Deveney *et al.* (1987) found the offender was a parental family member in 62 percent of the sexual abuse cases. In his study of male offenders, Robinson (1989) discovered that 41 percent were biological fathers, 24 percent stepfathers, 27 percent some other familial relations, and only 7 percent of the offenders were men from outside of the family structure. Although perpetrators are both male and female, the percentage of females is in the minority. Russell (1986) reported only 5 percent of offenders in her study to be female.

Russell also sheds light on the families of incest victims. In her study, there was no significant correlation of the father's education or occupation with the occurrence of abuse. There was also no significant correlation of abuse with mothers who worked in the labor force or with those who were homemakers. Incest victims were underrepresented in lower income families and slightly overrepresented in the highest income brackets. Race and ethnicity were likewise insignificant factors, with the exception of Asians, who reported significantly less abuse. In terms of religious upbringing, women raised as Jews were abused significantly less often than those raised Catholic or Protestant.

Symptoms of Sexual Abuse

The only indicator that is incontrovertible proof of sexual abuse is the presence of sexually transmitted diseases in young children. If a three year old has gonorrhea, this is the result of sexual abuse. However, this is only determined by medical evidence and is not an indication to which most are privy. Some victims exhibit few or no symptoms. These are the children who cope by becoming compliant, doing what they are told, and trying not to attract attention.

Some of the indicators listed below can be signs of other problems. Children of dysfunctional families, as well as those undergoing a particularly stressful time, may exhibit some of the same symptoms. It is also important to view behaviors and emotions within the context of normal childhood and adolescent psychosexual development. As mentioned, except for medical clues, there is no absolute proof of sexual abuse. However, if a number of these indicators are present and remain consistent over time, there is reason to consider the possibility of sexual abuse.

SIGNS AND INDICATORS
(compiled by Jeanne Wess)

I. Infants and Toddlers
A. Physical Signs
　　1. Trauma to genitals or mouth; genital or urinary irritation and/or venereal disease

2. Other bruises, burns, or injuries
3. Unexplained sore throats may indicate oral sex
4. Unusual or offensive odors, vaginal or penile discharge, and vaginal, penile or rectal bleeding or laceration
5. Complaints of discomfort or pain in the genital or rectal area
6. Foreign bodies in the vagina, urethra, or rectum.

B. Socio-Emotional Behavioral Signs
1. Intense fear of people in general or of a specific place or person
2. Abrupt changes in behavior
3. Sleep disturbances (bedwetting, nightmares, insomnia)
4. Withdrawal and/or depression
5. Developmental delays.

II. Preschool Children
All of the above signs and:
A. Physical Signs
1. Bedwetting
2. Wetting and/or soiling pants
3. Regressive behavior (e.g., thumbsucking)
4. Hyperactivity
5. Somatic complaints—chronic headaches, abdominal pain, constipation.

B. Socio-Emotional Behavioral Signs
1. Sudden changes in behavior
2. Child's direct or coded statement indicating sexual hurt.

C. Sexualized Behaviors
(These especially need to be considered in the light of normal sexual development.)
1. Excessive masturbation
2. Sexualized kissing, thrusting
3. Sexual acting out with siblings or peers
4. Precocious knowledge of sexual activity
5. Excessive sexual curiosity.

III. School-Aged Children
All of the above signs and:

1. Disturbed peer interactions
2. Change in school performance: inability to concentrate, drop in grades, tardiness, and truancy
3. Mistrust of adults in general
4. Depression, withdrawal, sadness, listlessness
5. Sleep disorders, such as nightmares, insomnia
6. Avoidance of physical activity and undressing.

IV. Adolescents

All of the above signs and:

1. Self-destructive activity and suicidal thoughts, self-inflicted injuries
2. Eating disorders
3. Delinquent behavior and/or running away
4. Drug and alcohol abuse
5. Early pregnancy
6. Prostitution, promiscuity, or other unusual sexual behaviors.

Sexual abuse virtually always occurs in a context of secrecy and helplessness. Abuse usually happens when the child is alone with the adult and the message, no matter how it is conveyed, is to keep the secret. Small wonder that children are reluctant to disclose abuse. Examine the messages children are given early in life: "Do what your parents tell you," "Listen to your uncle," or "Mind the babysitter." When the child trusts the adult who delivers the message, it is even more deeply ingrained.

Betrayal of this trust is the ultimate wound, as Charlene, a survivor, expresses so poignantly:

Remember when you were a child? Was there a special person in your life? A grandparent, uncle, or family friend? Someone who took you to carnivals, the movies, the park? Did you sit and talk for hours? Did you feel loved and important? How about trust—you never felt any fear, did you? Now imagine how you would have felt if that person touched you sexually. This person says that this is good, it is all right, "This is how you will know how much I love you." How is this making you feel right now? Feel it. Experience it, because this is how an abused child feels. Now add, "Don't tell anyone. This is our secret. If you tell, you won't be believed. If you tell, nobody will love you." As the abuse continues, this person causes you pain and tells you, "If you tell, there will be even more pain." How do you feel now? Are you confused, angry? Imagine how a child feels.

How does a young child cope with this dilemma? For a child to think of its parent as bad would be tantamount to abandonment. The parent must be seen as good. Thus, the only hope is to blame one's self. This creates co-existing feelings of love and hate which, to the victim and to others, can look and seem crazy. It is not. It is the only way the child can protect himself or herself from the painful reality in order to survive (Summitt, 1983).

Ultimately, the classic role reversal is apparent: the child is not only taking care of the parent's needs, but assumes the responsibility for the future of the family. "If you tell..." is a small phrase that successfully shifts the feelings of responsibility for subsequent consequences to the child.

Disclosure of Abuse

Disclosure of sexual abuse is one of the most difficult things for a child to do. Younger children may disclose accidentally, not realizing the implications of what they are saying. Older children tell in a more deliberate fashion, usually just wanting the abuse to stop and not being fully aware of the implications. Adolescents will sometimes angrily state it in the middle of a heated argument.

The task of telling is difficult for children for numerous reasons. In most instances, the child has been threatened that something negative will happen if she or he tells. The range of threats is wide. Some are subtle; some are not. "If you tell, I won't be your friend." "Your mother won't believe you." "I will go to jail." "I will kill you." Young children think literally. Therefore, a statement of anticipated violence is not understood as an idle threat but as a statement of fact.

Jane, age 14, disclosed a while ago that a good friend of her parents had been sexually abusing her for years. It was getting close to the time of the trial when she began to talk in therapy about not being able to testify. As the court date came closer, she began to run away. She was clearly terrified about the prospect of testifying in front of the offender. After returning from two weeks on the run, she painfully revealed to her therapist that the offender

had threatened physical harm to her mother if she told. She had
known him to be violent in the past and felt that it was up to her
to protect her mother.

The insidious, but often accurate, nature of the threats clearly
impedes disclosure. "If you tell, I will have to leave the house." "I
will go to jail." "You will have to move." "Your mother can't af-
ford to support you." In some cases, these prove to be true.

Guilt and embarrassment also impede a child from disclosing.
To discuss sexual issues is difficult for anyone. For a child to discuss sexual issues which he or she perceives as wrong is even
more difficult. The burden of guilt is often mistakenly assumed
by the victim.

It is important to be aware of general reactions, both the child's
and yours, and to know what to do if a child discloses to you. If
that happens, shock, anger and confusion are all normal reactions
on your part. You may have these strong feelings about what the
child has told you, but *it is important not to alarm the child with a
strong emotional response.* Use supervision or colleagues to process
your own feelings. If, for any reason, you find it too difficult to
talk to the child, get someone to help you or to do it for you. The
more familiar you are with the subject, the less likely you are to
overreact. Reading accounts of abuse is one way to desensitize
yourself.

There is a possibility that you will know the alleged offender.
This can be difficult, especially if you have positive feelings toward the person. Do not repeat Freud's mistake of making excus-
es for what happened, or revealing disbelief. If a child's disclosure
is met with disbelief, this only confirms to the child that there is
something wrong with him or her and the likelihood of telling
someone else in the future becomes negligible.

You can believe the child.   Nearly all children of any age tell the
truth when they disclose abuse, including teenagers. In fact, the
initial disclosure frequently underrepresents the extent of the
abuse. Most children will begin by telling some of what happened
to see what reaction they will elicit.

Deedee, age 5, was referred for therapy after a report had been
filed with the local protective service agency that her stepfather
had been fondling her. In the initial sessions, she revealed in her
play stories of the father doll touching the baby doll. It was only
after three months of treatment that she began to play out scenes

of the father doll performing oral sex with the young doll. When asked if anything like that had ever happened to her, she was able to talk about her stepfather coming into her bed at night and doing this to her.

If a child appears confused and does not relate events in a way that seems logical, this is understandable. Children do not have an adult sense of time and the trauma of the events can blur their memories. *Reassure the child and let the child know that he or she did the right thing in telling you.*

Do not press the child for details. Children may only be ready to discuss some parts of the abuse. Pushing too hard may only further frighten and confuse the child. It is not your job to gather all the facts in the case.

Let the child know that the abuse is not his or her fault. The child needs to know that the victim is never to blame. This is easier said than done because children often assume the responsibility.

When Carol was young, she liked to spend time in her father's workroom. She would often just sit and watch as he repaired small appliances. When she was 6 years old, he asked her to take off her clothes and he masturbated in front of her. The abuse continued over the next 8 years and progressed to fondling, "digital" penetration, and intercourse. After her disclosure at age 14, a recurrent theme in therapy was, "What did I do to make him do this? I don't know what I did but I must have done something."

Although it is important to let the child know that the offender is to blame, *be careful not to express negative feelings toward the offender.* Differentiate between the offender as a person and his or her behavior. Remember that 80 percent of abused children are abused by someone they know and they often have mixed feelings about the offender. Although a child may express anger at one moment, this does not necessarily represent all of his or her feelings for the offender.

Steven was 12 when he revealed to the school guidance counselor that his grandfather had been sexually abusing him for the past five years. This disclosure took place after he had had an argument with his grandfather. He expressed to the counselor both his anger about the fight as well as the abuse. The guidance counselor was outraged that Steve's own grandfather had abused him and expressed it. Steve bolted from the office and failed to return home. He was found by his father later that night hiding in the woods behind the school. He was sobbing and talking about how much he loved his grandfather.

When talking to a child, use the child's language and do not put words into a child's mouth. You may think you understand what the child is saying but the child's perception may not be the same as yours. When Julie, age 3, talked about her "bum" she was actually referring to her vagina. Katie, age 4, talked about the turtle she played with in the bathtub. In fact, the turtle was her uncle's penis.

Let the child know you will do your best to support him or her. Children need to be protected from further assault. Let them know you will need to tell other people who can help keep them safe. Do not make promises not to tell anyone what you have heard. Sexual abuse is a crime that is to be reported: laws of confidentiality do not apply. In the Catholic church, if a child tells a priest about abuse under the seal of confession, he should make every effort to talk to the child outside of the confessional.

To Do Nothing Is Wrong
Whether or not to report the suspicion of child sexual abuse is a question which has both legal and ethical implications. In the United States all fifty states have mandatory child abuse reporting laws. There are some differences in what professions are listed as mandated reporters, although physicians are mandatory reporters in all the states. In some states, the list expands to include teachers, counselors, daycare providers, nurses, clergy, and a variety of others. Check local regulations to see if you are mandated by law to file a report of abuse with the agency responsible for the protection of children in your state.

In addition to a potential legal mandate, however, ethical issues must be considered. To do nothing is wrong. If a child tells you that sexual abuse is occurring, it is usually because he or she wants the abuse to stop. Doing nothing allows it to continue, abandons the child, and reinforces the false notion that the abuse is the responsibility of the child.

When Lisa's mother found out that Lisa, age 14, was being sexually abused by her uncle, she took immediate steps to protect her. She allowed no further contact with the uncle and took Lisa to the local mental health agency for counseling. Because of state law, the therapist was a mandatory reporter, but she never followed through with her obligation to file a report. Instead, she encouraged the family to go to the police on their own. In a few weeks, Lisa began to refuse to go to therapy, but at her mother's urging finally reported the abuse to the police. The police filed the necessary report. When Lisa eventually developed a relationship with another therapist, she constantly blamed herself for her uncle serving time in jail. "If I had never told the police, this wouldn't have happened." If the first therapist had filed, she would have lifted some of the responsibility from Lisa.

In deciding whether or not to notify the child's parent(s) of a disclosure of abuse, there are numerous factors to consider; it may be important to seek consultation before acting. *The ruling consideration is the safety of the child.* If it appears that the child will be protected by the parents and that the parents have no vested emotional interest in the alleged offender, then it might be appropriate to tell them. This would occur in cases where the alleged offender is an outsider to the family, such as a babysitter, school teacher, scout leader or minister. If the offender is a priest or minister, however, some parents who are committed members of the congregation may have an emotional interest in keeping the reputation of the church leader untarnished.

If there is any reason to believe that the child would be put in further jeopardy as a result of informing the parent(s), you should not do so. This would usually apply if the alleged offender were a family member. For example, if the father were accused, it might seem possible to call the mother and have her protect the child. However, there is no way to predict whether the mother will believe the child or be emotionally able to protect the child.

In many situations, to inform the family too early in the process can create even greater pressure for the child to recant or change the story. You might assume the ability to anticipate how a particular family would react if you know the family members, but these reactions are not easy to predict. Dealing with such trauma throws the whole family into crisis and often people react differently than expected. Local agencies dealing with reports of sexual abuse handle these issues frequently. If you have questions, consult them.

Effects of Sexual Abuse

The impact which the abuse has upon a child is influenced by

several factors. In general, the closer the relationship with the offender, the more traumatic the abuse. The type of abuse, its duration, and the degree of violence involved, either real or perceived,
are all considerations when assessing the amount of damage done
to a child's psyche.

In recent years, the effects of sexual abuse have been viewed in
the context of post-traumatic stress disorder, (PTSD) a diagnostic
category listed in the DSM-III-R (American Psychiatric Association, 1987). Included in this category are the following disorders:

1. The person has experienced an event that would evoke significant symptoms of distress in almost anyone.

2. The trauma is re-experienced either through recurrent intrusive recollections, dreams, or feeling as if the traumatic event
were reoccurring.

3. There may be a numbing of responsiveness, efforts to avoid
thoughts associated with the abuse, diminished interest in activities, and feelings of estrangement from others.

4. At least two of the following set of symptoms need also be
present: sleep difficulties, irritability or outbursts of anger, difficulty concentrating, hypervigilance, exaggerated startle response,
and reaction to events that resemble an aspect of the trauma.

When a child has been sexually abused, he or she loses the ability to control the environment. It is as if the last barrier to security
and identity has been eroded and there are no boundaries and no
safe places. Basic trust in relationships has been shattered. *For the
abused child, the world is an unsafe place.*

In addition to the above-mentioned impacts, sexual abuse can
affect a child's perception of God and of the church. This writer
talked with several adults who had been abused as children. They
were asked to try to recapture feelings they had as children toward God and the church. Although some had few feelings on the
issue, the majority of responses clustered into two categories:
those whose perceptions were positive and those whose perceptions were negative.

The negative memories include perceptions of God and the
church as uncaring, using church teaching to blame one's self, and
expecting judgmental responses from clergy and religious. For example, when Barbara was 8, her mother remarried and the family
began to attend church. She became involved in the youth group.
Her stepfather drove her to these meetings and it was en route
that the abuse would occur. She felt that the church was a sham

and a mockery. "I had to be sweet when I wasn't feeling that way....I was hoping there was a God but I felt there wasn't."

The concept of God that develops in children can often be related to a projection of feelings for authority figures. For example, Fran said that by the time she was 13 years old she knew her family was insane and thus deduced that God must also be insane. Both of her parents were alcoholic. Her mother sexually abused her as a youngster, her father during her adolescent years. She also had a particularly hard time with the fourth commandment. "How was I supposed to honor my father and mother," Fran said, "when they were both sexually abusing me?"

God was viewed by several victims as punishing and judgmental. Marilyn said, "My perception of God was one of fear. I believed that if I did the right things, I'd have a good life. So when the abuse started, I was shocked." She was raised in a small town in the southern United States in a family with a fundamentalist Baptist background. "At an early age, I tried to question and say there were things that I didn't believe, but there was a lot of pressure to join the church and be baptized. Those who wouldn't, would go to hell. I obeyed everyone older; I did what anybody told me." This type of pressure and rigid obedience to authority can set the stage for abuse.

Self-concept is often shattered by childhood abuse. Laurie told me, "I felt that if you're good, good things happen and if you're bad, bad things happen. The abuse by my cousin started after my father left, when I was four. I knew I had done something wrong and I deserved it."

According to Beth, another victim, "I could never look at the altar, especially around the ages of 11–13; I didn't feel like I was good enough to look up. Part of me thought the devil was inside of me because of the thoughts I would have sometimes."

Some victims of abuse were fearful and mistrusting of clergy and religious and expected a judgmental response to a disclosure of the abuse. "You could never tell because they would blame you." "I was terrified what they would think of me if they knew." "My minister was okay as a person but I would never tell him anything about it."

Sometimes their mistrusting perceptions are justified: Laurie was feeling suicidal as an adolescent and was trying to tell the priest not only what she was feeling but about the abuse that caused it. She recalls beginning her story and after the first sentence being told that killing is the ultimate sin and that her body was sacred. "I went to him for hope," she said, "not for a guilt-trip."

On the other hand, some of the adult survivors of childhood sexual abuse had positive perceptions of the church and of God. They viewed them as a refuge and a sign of hope. Beth wrote, "I used to talk to God on my back in my bed at night. It seemed all right to talk to Him in the dark so He couldn't see me; I thought He might mix me up with someone else and answer my prayers."

Charlene used to pray to God while the abuse was occurring. "It was my way of gaining some comfort. As an adult, I know that it was the way that I dissociated from the experience; but as a child, all I knew was that I got strength from praying to God."

Charlene was able to recognize that it was not religion that was "bad," but religion could be abused by some people. Her perception of the clergy and religious was a positive one. "I attended a Catholic high school and one day the principal called me in and said I would be staying there as a boarder. It was a place of refuge for me. I think some of them knew something was wrong. They never asked because I don't think they knew how to handle it; but they gave me kindness and acceptance. I felt cared for. That Christmas, I stayed there with a few students who were from other countries and who couldn't go home. It was the first Christmas I ever enjoyed. It was a peaceful time."

Life for Fran was composed of two extremes. Both of her parents were alcoholic and both sexually abused her. During all this time, she attended parochial school. "The church represented safety and protection. I used to hate vacations. School was a safe haven; there was heat, food and organization to my day. They saved me; they gave me life skills and a conscience. I had great devotion to the Blessed Mother; it was as if she was the mother that I didn't have."

Summary

In communicating and dealing with any group of children or adolescents, one must assume that some have been, or are being, sexually abused. As best we know, there are more girls abused than boys. There are very few other distinctions with regard to social class, race, ethnicity, or educational background. One of the few differences is that Christians tend to be abused more frequently than are Jews.

The ability to recognize the signs and symptoms of sexual abuse is an important skill. Clusters of the indicators alert us to the probability of problems of some sort. If, either spontaneously or upon gentle questioning, a child discloses that he or she is being sexually abused, the reaction given will influence the rest of the process. Emotional and physical protection are essential.

Disclosure creates a crisis for the entire family. If the abuse has been occurring within the family, breaking the secrecy upsets the family balance and often raises divided loyalties. It is crucial that the child receive support during this process. Also, he or she should receive therapy as soon as possible to deal with the trauma. This is not to negate the parents' need for help, but to emphasize that the child is the victim of this crime and has the immediate need for attention.

The religious attitudes and values of abused children are influenced by the manner in which they understand the teachings of the church, their perception of the clergy and religious, and how they interrelate these values and perceptions with their experience as victims. This is an area that should be explored in more detail (Sargent, 1989). However, our initial awareness and understanding of child sexual abuse can help us to re-examine church attitudes and social programs. Such a re-examination might lead to a continuing improvement in the quality of care we provide for the victims and their families of this societal tragedy.

References

American Psychiatric Association *Diagnostic and Statistical Manual of Mental Disorders.* Third Edition, Revised. Washington, D.C.: APA, 1987.

Deveney, W., B. Raab-Protentis, D. Rintell, and J. Starr. "Services to Sexually Abused Children and Their Families—Part II: Characteristics of Children and Families in Treatment." Boston: Department of Social Services/Office for Professional Services/Research, Evaluation and Planning Unit, 1987.

Finkelhor, D. *Sexually Victimized Children*. New York: Free Press, 1979.

_____. *Child Sexual Abuse: New Theory and Research*. New York: Free Press, 1984.

_____. *A Sourcebook on Child Sexual Abuse*. Beverly Hills: Sage Publications, 1986.

Herman, J. *Father-Daughter Incest*. Cambridge, Massachusetts: Harvard University Press, 1981.

Kinsey, A., *et al*. *Sexual Behavior in the Human Female*. Philadelphia: W.B. Saunders, 1953.

National Center on Child Abuse and Neglect. *Study Findings: Study of National Incidence and Prevalence of Child Abuse and Neglect*. Washington, D.C.: U.S. Department of Health and Human Services, 1980 and 1988.

Robinson, D. "A Brief Summary and Bibliography on Child Sexual Abuse in the Family." Massachusetts Society for the Prevention of Cruelty to Children, 1989.

_____. "Evaluating Intrafamilial Child Sexual Abuse Treatment: Group Process and Outcomes in Multi-Site Programs." Doctoral Dissertation, Harvard University, 1989.

Russell, D. *The Secret Trauma*. New York: Basic Books, Inc., 1986.

Sargent, N. "Spirituality and Adult Survivors." In *Vulnerable Populations*. Edited by S. Sgroi. Lexington, Massachusetts: Lexington Books, 1989.

Summitt, R. "The Child Sexual Abuse Accommodation Syndrome." *Child Abuse and Neglect* 7 (1983):177–193.

Wess, J. "Signs and Indicators of Child Sexual Abuse." In *Child Sexual Abuse: An Interdisciplinary Professional Reference Manual*. Worcester Area Child Sexual Abuse Task Force, 1987.

From Victim to Survivor:
The Treatment of Adults
Who Have Been Sexually Abused as Children

Mollie Brown, R.S.M., R.N., Ph.D.

When Sister "Ruth" came to us at Spirit House, a therapeutic community for women religious, her behavior was rigid and controlling. She told everyone how to pray and expected them to follow suit. She constantly wore a full religious habit and expected no one to be seen without theirs. Her attitude toward the community was critical and judgmental when they, inevitably, did not live up to her perfectionist ideas. She needed to be in control.

On the other hand, Ruth was secretive about her private life. In our small group sessions, Ruth shared little about herself. After several months, no one had gotten close to her. She put others at a distance and kept her interior world "safe" through her perfectionism, rigidity, and control. But, she was very much alone.

The truth was that Sister Ruth was a victim of childhood sexual abuse. She was molested in turn by her father, brother and uncles. For Ruth, as well as for other victims of childhood sexual abuse, the world became an unsafe place. The rigidity, perfectionism, and control were merely defenses against feeling the enormous trauma that lay within.

Slowly, and with much hard work, Ruth began to let go of some of her rigidity and the demands she placed upon others. Her inner world also began to loosen up; as a sign of this change, she would occasionally appear in the community dressed in informal clothes. And she began to share little things about herself in the small group sessions. These changes might appear to be small, but for her, they were arduous and important steps forward.

Initially, when she began to open up to other members of the community, Sister Ruth was frightened. She expected to receive disgust and rejection. But she was surprised to find that people still liked her and stayed with her. Eventually, she shared the dark, inner horror of her history of abuse. She also joined a self-help group called Survivors of Incest Anonymous. Finally, Sister Ruth returned to her community and is currently on the road to a new life as a survivor of incest, not as its victim.

In years past at Spirit House, the most common "presenting problem" of women religious was depression. But in recent times, a new presenting problem has dominated our work: childhood sexual abuse in women religious. Approximately one-half of those now entering our therapeutic community are suffering from such abuse.

It is commonly thought that one out of three or four women in North America is sexually abused by age 18. This ratio may be even higher among women vowed to a religious life. But the most important truth of this chapter is that adults who have been sexually abused as children do not have to stay *victims*. They do, like Sister Ruth, have a choice to emerge as *survivors* with new strength, new understanding, and new compassion.

Until the late 1970s, little research had been done on sexual abuse, incest, and the enduring symptoms with which victims lived. Those years of silence have been referred to as the "Age of Denial." This phrase aptly described the lack of awareness of and the lack of treatment for the victims of child molestation. The women's movement and television dramas portraying sexual abuse gave children, their parents, and adult survivors the courage to begin speaking their truth.

Even with such initial encouragement, survivors still suffered yet another trauma; it is called the "second injury." Butler (1978) used this term to describe the pain when no assistance comes from agencies or individuals to whom the victim turns for help. The pain of this "second injury" results from the repeated lack of validation or assistance from adults to whom the truth of the abuse is confided. This leads to the victim developing a personal identity that is based on shame.

Bradshaw (1988) states that such a shame-based identity is paralyzing to the child's development. He believes that unless intense psychological work is done to move out of that shame, the individual will never be able to face the world freely. And, in order to move out of this shame, the victim must deal with at least two levels of distrust: the trust violated by the perpetrator of the crime, and the trust violated by the adult from whom the child had a right to expect help.

Post-traumatic Stress Disorder

Courtois (1988) and her colleagues, as early as 1981, decided that post-traumatic stress disorder was the most appropriate classification for what they were seeing at the Cleveland State University Counseling Center. At that time, such a classification was reserved for Vietnam veterans. However, it also applied to their students who had been sexually molested as children.

The Diagnostic and Statistical Manual of Mental Disorders (DSM III-R, 1987) lists criteria that are necessary to use a given classification. Post-traumatic stress disorder (PTSD) clearly fits the symptoms of the adult survivor. Criteria for PTSD include some of the following:

1. The person has experienced an event that is outside the range of usual human experience and that would be markedly distressing to almost everyone.

2. The traumatic experience is persistently re-experienced in at least one of the following ways: a) recurrent and intrusive recollections of the event; b) recurrent distressing dreams of the event; c) sudden acting or feeling as if the traumatic event were recurring...; d) intense psychological distress at exposure to events that symbolize or represent an aspect of the traumatic event, including anniversaries of the trauma.

3. Persistent avoidance of stimuli associated with the trauma or numbing of general responsiveness (not present before the trauma) as indicated by at least three of the following: a) efforts to avoid thoughts or feelings associated with the trauma; b) efforts to avoid activities or situations that arouse recollections of the trauma; c) inability to recall an important aspect of the trauma (psy-

chogenic amnesia); d) markedly diminished interest in significant activities...; e) feeling of detachment or estrangement from others; f) restricted sense of affect; g) sense of a foreshortened future, e.g., does not expect to have a career, marriage, children, or a long life.

4. Persistent symptoms of increased arousal (not present before the trauma) as indicated by at least two of the following: a) difficulty falling or staying asleep; b) irritability or outbursts of anger; c) difficult concentrating; d) hypervigilance; e) exaggerated startle response; f) physiologic reactivity upon exposure to events that symbolize or resemble an aspect of the traumatic event (DSM III-R, 1987).

Kathy came from a family where the rule was that the youngest female child was "fair game" for all male relatives. From earliest memory, she was abused by her father, uncles, and brothers. Her mother was aware of the abuse but she, too, had been the youngest female child in her family. In a "second injury," Kathy's mother afforded her no protection. Instead, Kathy was given the message that this was the way things were and that she should be grateful that things were not worse.

At the age of 16, Kathy came into our counseling office. She was vague, spoke hesitatingly, and could remember little. At times, she would hyperventilate, yet her expression was so bland that it was difficult to understand what was happening to her. The hyperventilation would be followed by a "dissociation" where Kathy's consciousness would split away from her painful memories. Then, she would retreat into a world she had created in order to feel safe.

As Kathy began treatment, it became clear that she had no plans for her future. If she lived, she would make enough money to eat. But, she had no hopes or plans for anything more.

Kathy was suffering from a post-traumatic stress disorder as outlined in the DSM III-R. Being sexually abused by one's father, uncles and brothers is truly an experience that "would be markedly distressing to almost anyone." As the recollections of the abuse came into her mind, she experienced "intense psychological distress" marked by the hyperventilation and then her dissociation. The latter was an effort "to avoid thoughts or feelings associated with the trauma." Kathy's blank look manifested her "detachment from others." Finally, her lack of future plans and hopes stemmed from her "sense of a foreshortened future." She did not expect to have a long life or a hope-filled future.

Some Signs of Childhood Abuse in Adults
Some ways of alerting oneself to the possibility that one may be living or working with an adult victim of sexual abuse is to look at the four aspects of the human personality: relational, physical, social and spiritual. These categories are not mutually exclusive. For example, any discussion of a survivor's spirituality is closely related to his or her ways of relating to others. And since a victim relates with and through the body, the physical and social are also intertwined. However, these categories give us a way of thinking about the many and varied symptoms that an adult survivor of sexual abuse may display.

Relational Problems
One characteristic relational problem of an adult survivor is a feeling of emptiness in life. This is sometimes referred to as a lack of *élan* or *joie de vivre*. Talking with such victims, one can feel a lack of responsiveness or resonance in their personalities. For example, Kathy had no goals, no future, and had a blank look on her face. Her life felt empty.

In spite of the "blank stare," there is no denying the anger and rage that can flare up in a victim. Frequently, there is no way of identifying the stimulus for the rage, nor can the person identify its cause. A psychogenic amnesia may block any awareness or recollection of the underlying cause. The victim may be totally unaware of the psychic injury.

However, other people often become fearful of the victim's intense rage. They will likely withdraw from that person for their own safety or comfort. This withdrawal of others creates, in a victim, a sense of abandonment and isolation, which further compounds the injury. This, in turn, may trigger yet another bout of anger. It leads to a cyclical pattern of injury-rage-isolation.

When this pattern begins, the victim may withdraw from others and start to *"act in."* "Acting in" is putting oneself down before others and using an inner, destructive, self-talk to condemn oneself. This destructive self-talk may be externally symbolized by the victims cutting themselves, burning themselves, making suicidal gestures, or engaging in other self-punishing behaviors. "Acting in" is more frequently observed in women than in men. Men are more likely to "act out." Thus, they may become delinquent, destructive, abusive, or even homicidal. This "acting in" or "acting out" reinforces the victim's shame-based identity and tightens the downward spiral.

Since the ordinary events of everyday life may be reminders of trauma, the victim tries to maintain a safe environment so that nothing triggers painful memories of the past. Hence, all facets of the victim's life must be under control. While it may be possible to control inanimate objects, most people are unwilling to be controlled. Since control is thought to be imperative for the victim's safety, and other people refuse to be controlled, the victim panics. The panic is then converted to rage and the vicious cycle continues.

Physical Problems

The adult victim will not only try to control her interpersonal relations, she will also try to control her *physical dimensions*. Characteristically, she may be involved in addictions, eating disorders, or obesity. For example, a female child who was sexually molested by an adult male may have been told by her mother that she "asked for it." The child will soon learn that if one is fat and ugly, one will be safe because men do not like fat ladies. Hence, to be fat is not to "ask for it" any more.

When Sister Joan came into treatment, she was obese. As a child, she had been frequently abused by her paternal grandfather. Her father was actively alcoholic and her mother was diagnosed with multiple physical problems related to stress. In treatment, Joan finally said, "I've kept this secret so long, it has made me sick. I won't be sick any longer!" As she began to face the dysfunction of her incestuous and alcoholic family, Joan began to lose weight and to return to her own shape.

While obesity may be one victim's way out, anorexia or bulimia may be another's. Refusing to eat, or eating and purging, are ways a woman may use to control her body. This feeling of control over the body is important for a woman who was not in control of it during her abuse. Though these kinds of "acting in" behaviors are self-destructive and can be fatal, the adult survivor is blinded by an overwhelming desire to feel in control of her body.

Other adult survivors may develop an addiction to drugs and/ or alcohol in an attempt to quiet the memories and the pain. If psychogenic amnesia is not enough, drugs and alcohol may be used to dull the mind. Sometimes survivors will deliberately use drugs and alcohol; other times, they will merely fall into the dysfunctional patterns of their families: drug and alcohol abuse is common in victims' families.

When "acting in" fails to control the inner torment, the victim may move to "acting out" in the wider, social dimension of her life.

Social Symptoms

The social symptoms of adult survivors may range from extreme withdrawal and isolation to behaviors that rebel against society. Jakubiak (1987) states that incest, or any sexual abuse, is a violation of trust. Children trust the adults in their lives to protect them. Fundamentally, it is the violation of this trust that constitutes the great trauma of incest. It would not be unreasonable to expect the survivors to "act out" in rebellious ways. Sometimes it is done consciously, but most often the motive is hidden, even from the survivor.

For example, drugs are not only a way of forgetting the pain, they are also a means of rebelling against the adults who failed the child. Sexual acting out and promiscuity can likewise be acts of rebelling against family and society. They may also be attempts on the part of the victims to control who uses their bodies, and when their bodies are "used," rather than risk being at the whim of an abuser.

Spiritual Symptoms

All of the above categories: relational, physical and social, cannot but impinge upon the spiritual dimension of the victim. A child's image and understanding of God is built upon the significant adults in her life.

Thus, it is not uncommon for victims to report an inability to pray. Also, women victims who have been abused by men often have difficulty dealing with any masculinity in God. In an attempt to run from any semblance of the masculine, they may go to the other extreme and relate to God only as feminine. In a similar way, some survivors cannot relate to Jesus because of his masculinity.

If a child learns that adults cannot be trusted, it is highly unlikely that he or she will learn to trust God. If a girl's experience is that no one believes her and her identity is shame-based, she will be filled with fear before an unknown God. Without having developed a sense of integrity and values as guides for the spiritual journey, the survivor may feel spiritually abandoned or lost.

Characteristic Symptoms of Childhood Sexual Abuse in Adults

Personal/Relational Symptoms
- lack of *élan* or *joie de vivre*
- psychogenic amnesia concerning childhood events
- suicidal thoughts and/or gestures
- self-mutilation (e.g., cutting, burning, maiming oneself)
- rigid or controlling behavior
- depression and/or anxiety
- low self-esteem, inability to trust others

Physical Symptoms
- alcohol/drug abuse or addiction
- sexual disorders (e.g. frigidity or sexual addictions)
- eating disorders (e.g., obesity, anorexia, bulimia)
- gastrointestinal problems (e.g., abdominal pains, appetite disorders, constipation)
- skeletal muscle tension (e.g., headaches, back pains, chest pains, tension in legs or arms)
- disturbed sleep

Social Symptoms
- isolation or withdrawal
- delinquent or anti-social behavior
- homicidal impulses or actions
- sexually acting out (e.g., promiscuity)
- compulsive achieving
- workaholism

Spiritual Symptoms
- inability to pray
- irrational fear of God
- sense of impending punishment by God for unknown reasons
- unable to relate to masculinity in God or Jesus because he is male (in females abused by males)
- lack of direction for spiritual journey; feeling lost or hopeless

In short, the adult who was molested as a child may display any number of symptoms that indicate an underlying, traumatic stress. It should be noted that all of the above are possible symptoms, not only of child sexual abuse in adult survivors, but also of a variety of other disorders. Such symptoms may also be signs of an underlying cause of a post-traumatic stress disorder other than childhood sexual abuse. However, when such signs occur, one should be alert to the possibility of sexual abuse in the individual's history.

Some Issues in Treatment

Because sexual abuse affects all the dimensions of a person's life—relational, physical, social and spiritual—all of these areas need to be addressed in treatment.

Rebuilding Trust   Since the most damaging aspect of childhood sexual abuse is a betrayal of trust, the most important aspect of treatment is rebuilding that trust. Any move that will enable victims to see that they can trust adults, without being misused by them, will begin the bridge-building necessary for healing. It is important that the victims learn that, although they were coerced into submitting to childhood abuse, they no longer need to submit to being misused. The therapist's modeling of healthy behavior that respects the rights of others can be a powerful witness for the victims. They need to learn that there can be another way of living.

The age at which an individual has been abused will have an effect on his or her development. If the abuse happened before the child reached puberty, a "precognitive belief system" may be locked into the adult victim's perceptions of his or her environment. For example, *children are naturally self-centered and see themselves as responsible for events beyond their control.* Adults abused as children are likely to feel responsible for the abuse. They are filled with self-blame and a low self-esteem. The therapist will want to encourage survivors to develop a healthier belief system and to rebuild their sense of self-esteem.

If the victim is a girl abused in her teens, she usually has a more developed belief system and can use these more mature beliefs in dealing with the abuse and its subsequent stress-related symptoms. As she builds a sense of trust in her therapist, she can more easily disclose the traumas and move beyond them.

If, however, the abused girl is developmentally disabled, she will have a more difficult time rebuilding trust in others. A major task in working with the developmentally impaired is helping them to learn that they can trust their caregivers. In such cases, depending on the degree of retardation, it may not be helpful to have the individual disclose events of the trauma. The attempt to remember and reconstruct the abuse may prove to be too stressful for the victim. In the long run, the major therapeutic task remains the same: the rebuilding of trust.

It is preferable to begin the treatment of the victim as close to the time of the abuse as possible. Some survivors say that the therapeutic process takes as long as the interval between the abuse and the start of treatment. With an early entrance into treatment, further incidences of revictimizations may be decreased or eliminated. In addition, the longer the time lapse between the trauma and the treatment, the more life history there will be to re-examine and reframe. Memories of past trauma and maladaptive behaviors developed to protect the individual from further abuse have to be addressed and abandoned for a healthier lifestyle.

Moving From Victim to Survivor

Adult decisions made when the survivor was not yet treated, and was thus living in a maladaptive mode, will have to be looked at from a healthier perspective. The relationships the individual developed as a *victim* will have to be renegotiated as she becomes a *survivor*. Earlier career decisions made as a victim will have to be reassessed since the reasons for choosing a career may no longer be present or useful. The individual will have to ask, "Why did I choose this lifestyle or job?" "Why do I choose to stay?" "Can I stay?" "Will I stay?"

The appropriateness of one's previous vocational choice is especially important for women religious. Some victims choose celibacy because it appears to be "safe"; they believe they will not have to enter into intimate relationships or deal with men whom they cannot trust. There are others who choose an environment of discipline and goodness to atone for their "dirty sins and secrets."

From recent work with male clergy, it is evident that some of them also have been abused and may have chosen celibacy for a similar reason: it appears to be a "safe" option. A short time ago, a priest came into our counseling office in a panic. He had been abused as a child and further abused as an adolescent. He chose to enter the seminary because he would be spared having to establish any potentially dangerous relationships. When he discovered, after ordination, that parishioners wanted to relate to him as a human being who was a priest, rather than relate only to his role, he panicked. At that point, the only option that he could perceive was to leave the active ministry. Long, slow, sometimes tedious work allowed him to see that he had other options.

Jakubiak (1987) discusses women religious whose choice of a celibate lifestyle was a free one, despite their history of victimization. They struggled with their past trauma and felt authentically called to religious life. In the light of a healthier perspective, they re-examined their original choice and confirmed it with a fuller heart.

All people's reasons for a vocational choice change from one life stage to another. Just as the victim will need to ask, "Why do I stay?" so, too, does everyone need to review earlier vocational choices. As survivors come to see their dysfunctional patterns, they are tempted to believe that everything they did since the time of the abuse has been worthless. The therapist will need to work closely with the survivor so that he or she can learn that earlier, less free choices do not invalidate everything that has been done during the intervening years. The therapist will want to assist the person to see that he or she is no longer a victim, but a survivor. As a survivor, the person is like everyone else: a survivor of life's many traumas.

A further issue in treatment is the sex of the victim and the sex of the abuser. The abuse of a female by another female may well have implications for the victim's future sexual orientation. Jakubiak (1987) mentions that females who have a lesbian orientation may be identifying with the male as a means of defending themselves against further abuse. As the women progress in treatment, it will be necessary to address their sexual orientation and their choice of lifestyle. Similarly, a male victim, abused by another male, may make life choices that will keep him safe. One issue in treatment will be an examination of those choices. Either a change to match his new understanding or a reaffirmation of the choice in freedom may be required.

Intimacy

Regardless of the sex of the victim and the abuser, a major issue in any treatment of sexual abuse is intimacy. Individuals who have been abused, as children or as adults, have experienced a traumatic blow to their ability to trust and, thus, their ability to be intimate. They find that they are unable to open themselves, in an intimate way, to another person. Such victims will do additional violence to themselves to see that they are closed and protected from other human beings and any possibility of further abuse. This violence may include such behaviors as dissociation, control, promiscuity, obesity, or substance abuse.

Intimacy, then, becomes an experience to avoid at all costs. A slow, careful movement on the part of the therapist to listen, to care, and to believe the client, can be the beginning of an experience of trust and then of intimacy. The therapist will be reticent to touch the survivor, since such physical contact may be associated with the original abuse and panic the client. A new understanding of intimacy needs to develop in which there is closeness and love without necessitating physical contact. The careful nurturing of this experience of intimacy is the foundation of a new, healthier life for the survivor.

The Healing Process
In light of the pain and trauma discussed above, it is important that the therapist have some frame of reference from which to work with the client. There are so many issues, so many side effects, that one needs to put them in order to ensure that the client has the full opportunity for healing.

One such frame of reference is Courtois's (1988) ten goals for treatment. These ten goals cover an early, middle and extended treatment plan that can be most helpful, while leaving sufficient latitude for the therapist's style and the client's particular needs.

Ten Goals for Treatment
1. Development of a commitment to treatment and the establishment of a therapeutic alliance
2. Acknowledgment and acceptance of the occurrence of the incest
3. Recounting the incest
4. Breakdown of feelings of isolation and stigma
5. The recognition, labeling and expression of feelings
6. Resolution of responsibility and survival issues
7. Grieving
8. Cognitive restructuring of distorted beliefs and stress responses
9. Self-determination and behavioral change
10. Education and skill-building (Courtois, 1988)

Bass and Davis (1988) list fourteen steps of the healing process, all of which are encompassed in Courtois's list. Other therapists have designed their own approaches to the problem and all spell out the same basic principles (Scurfield, 1985; Harris, 1986). Within all these approaches, the therapist acknowledges that healing is a process. Such a process cannot be forced into a time frame that will not fit the client. At times, the client may even need to take a vacation from the formal process.

However, the full process of healing must begin with the new experience of a trusting relationship with another adult. This other person must not allow herself or himself to be victimized by the victim. For example, it is not uncommon for adult victims to be verbally abusive, controlling, and manipulative in therapy. It is important that the therapist set limits in the therapeutic relationship. This kind of modeling of appropriate boundaries cannot be too highly stressed. It is in this healthy, respectful relationship of therapist and client, where trust does not lead to abuse, that the client may begin to learn self-determination and free choice.

There is always the question of which form of therapy is most useful: individual, therapeutic group, or self-help group. The answer is that all three models are useful, and perhaps necessary, at different times in the healing process. The individual therapy experience is essential for the development of a healthy, trusting, adult relationship. On the other hand, there is a point where clients need the feedback of a group of other survivors who have been where they have been. The "neurosis of uniqueness," of which Harry Stack Sullivan speaks, can be put to rest in the context of the group. The knowledge that the survivor is not unique is a great relief and an important step in the healing process.

Courtois's goals are not always neat and tidy. While the client takes a "vacation" from formal treatment, he or she still needs to maintain a foothold on the ascent to health. The twelve-step program that deals with incest survivors, Survivors of Incest Anonymous (SIA), can be especially useful.

One of SIA's customs is to exchange phone numbers with other members in case of an emergency. To have someone at the other end of the phone frequently saves the survivor from a panic attack. In SIA, members select a sponsor to guide them through the program. This is an opportunity to develop another trusting relationship with an adult. Such opportunities to bond with others broaden the repertoire of new behaviors and social contacts.

Conclusion

The widespread effects of childhood sexual abuse in the church make it a critical issue. The percentage of women religious who have been sexually abused is not known, but it is likely to be significantly higher than the 25–33 percent reported in the wider society of women. Likewise, we are seeing more priests and male religious who are also suffering the effects of childhood sexual abuse. It is our hope that the church, and our society, will face the wounds of the people and offer their support and resources for healing.

Interestingly, the church of the 1960s taught the anatomy and physiology of human sexuality. What was missing was a mature understanding of the emotional aspect of sexuality and the centrality of a loving, intimate relationship. In a magazine article a few years ago, a large number of women were interviewed and asked what they preferred: sex or intimacy. The overwhelming response was intimacy.

Women know they want intimacy. They want to be able to share. They want to be able to be held and to hold. They desire, more than anything, a truly intimate relationship built upon trust and respect. Only after that, if it is appropriate, do they want to consummate the relationship in a genital way.

We have recently discovered the epidemic proportions of sexual abuse in our society. In addition to dealing with the symptoms of the problem, a course of primary prevention is needed. Beyond the physiology of sex, we need to understand that the deepest longing of every human person is not to be genitally active, but to be truly intimate. In concentration camps, two men on either side of a barbed wire fence can be deeply intimate, without touching each other. To be intimate is to have the courage to know and to be known.

In treatment, adult survivors must face the specters of sexual abuse, rejection, abandonment, the pain of recovery, and the ever-present fear that what did happen might happen again. These specters must be dealt with in the light of day and put to rest. Such a journey can take a long time. And it is a journey that cannot be taken alone. Individuals must find a companion on the journey from victim to survivor. They must come out of the dark of secrets too horrible to be spoken, and find, in the light of day, a future to be anticipated and free.

Unless we seek to heal ourselves and our society, our "toxic shame gets more toxic," in the words of John Bradshaw. The cost of such treatment is high. A primary prevention program and re-education in intimacy and human sexuality will also be expensive. But it is not nearly as high as the cost of silence.

References

American Psychiatric Association. *Diagnostic and Statistical Manual of Mental Disorders*. Third edition, revised. Washington, D.C.: APA, 1987.

Bass, E. and L. Davis. *The Courage to Heal. A Guide for Women Survivors of Child Sexual Abuse*. New York: Harper & Row, 1988.

Bradshaw, J. *Healing the Shame That Binds You*. Deerfield Beach, Florida: Health Communications, 1988.

Butler, S. *Conspiracy of Silence: The Trauma of Incest*. New York: Bantam Books, 1978.

Courtois, C. *Healing the Incest Wound: Adult Survivors in Therapy*. New York: W.W. Norton & Company, 1988.

Harris, J.M. "A Model Training Seminar for Incest Survivors." Paper presented at the Fourth National Conference on the Sexual Victimization of Children, Children's Hospital National Medical Center, New Orleans, 1986.

Jakubiak, M., and S. Murphy. "Incest Survivors in Women's Communities," *Human Development* 8:2 (1987), 19–25.

Maltz, W. and B. Holman. *Incest and Sexuality: A Guide to Understanding and Healing*. Lexington, Massachusetts: Lexington Books, 1987.

Scurfield, R.M. "Post-trauma stress assessment and treatment: Overview and formulations." In C.R. Figley (ed.) *Trauma and Its Wake: The Study of Treatment of Post-traumatic Stress Disorder*. New York: Brunner/Mazel, 1985.

Survivors of Incest Anonymous (formerly Sexual Abuse Anonymous) P.O. Box 21817, Baltimore, MD 21222-6817.

A Priest Child Abuser Speaks

Anonymous

(Editor's Note: *The following is a contribution by a priest convicted of child sexual abuse. We are indebted to him for his courage and honesty in sharing his experience.*)

I was convicted in the 1980s and spent 14 months in a minimum security prison. I know one priest who got 20 years of hard labor. They wanted to make an example of him.

When I went to prison I had this Cinderella view: I thought I was going to be "corrected." Everyone knows that to correct child sex abusers they should be given some psychological treatment with a behavioral group setting to make sure that the behavior is well exhumed, well looked at, and modified so that it will never happen again.

But when I got to prison, there was nothing. No program at all—just the hate, the disdain, the purely cruel stuff with people looking at you saying, "There's that priest diddler." That comment would blast me out of the water for several days. I never liked directly facing what I was. It filled me with fear because it was the very thing I did not want to be. I wanted to put it as far away from me as I could. I just could not have done this.

I knew that in my true character I was not the person who would have acted this way. My true character would not have done that. So the lie of my life became apparent. I had a lot of trouble accepting that lie, that I was a child abuser. I would just go back and spend my days in my room.

I pretty much kept to myself. I learned to mind my own business. I am small of stature so I had to stay out of everyone's way because I do not have the muscle power to push someone out of the way if he is coming after me. There was one person who was a pretty bad guy. He hated me. He never laid a hand on me because he would have been sent back to a maximum security jail if he had, so he kept his distance. Eventually, however, he was released and he lived close to the place where I worked during the day (I was on a work release program). He saw me and tried to run me over with his car. The mocking and the hatred can change you.

No one, of course, ever killed me. But they toyed with me. Once, the lieutenant told me to move in upstairs with this huge man. I went upstairs and stood there in front of him. He said, "What are you doing here?" My heart was pounding 300 miles an hour because I knew this guy could chew me up and spit me out. I said, "The lieutenant told me that I was going to live here." "Well," he said, "you go back downstairs and tell the lieutenant that you're not coming in this room." I was intimidated enough to go downstairs to the security office and tell the lieutenant. He said, "Since when does he make the rules around here?" The other officers laughed. When they sent me up they knew he was not going to like it. They toyed with me.

I had to be on guard. But there were people I got along with. I became friendly with one of my roommates who was in for involuntary manslaughter. He asked to have me room with him. He was a nice guy. I was attracted to him from the beginning. He was neat in appearance and it looked like he had some gray matter between his ears. I had been living with another child molester in a different room. I did not like him. I did not like him at all.

I got along well with most of the guards. I think a lot of them felt pretty comfortable with me. They knew I was not going to do anything that would put them in any kind of jeopardy. There was only one, a lieutenant, who had it in for me. I think he had it in for everyone; he was filled with anger and out to hang everyone.

One day I was late coming home from work release. It was Good Friday. I had called and told another lieutenant that I would be late but he failed to tell this lieutenant, the one who was out to get me. When I got back from work release, the desk officer said, "Where have you been? The lieutenant is out looking for you." My heart sank.

When the lieutenant returned, he called me into his office and told me, "You're lugged, buddy. Pack your bags. You're out of here. You're not staying in this house." There were the handcuffs on his desk. At that point two officers came in to clear me out and put me in a maximum security prison or wherever they could find a place to just drop me off.

The other officers were pretty sympathetic. They could not understand why he was biting into this and hanging onto it. He would not accept my story until he finally got the thorn out of his paw and decided to call the other lieutenant who said, "Oh yeah, he called in to say he was going to be late." I received no apology. I just stood there until another officer asked if I could go.

It was the most hellish and scariest thing I ever faced...the disdain and the hatred I got. It was the first time in my life that I knew I was so out of control and I was a victim of a very vicious system that did not care a hoot or holler who I was or what I was or where I was. I did not even know what they were going to do with me. It was the toughest Good Friday I ever went through. It was black, really black. There was nothing left for me to hold on to.

I found out later that the lieutenant who was out to get me had been chasing his girlfriend's daughter around the house. His girlfriend publicly laid him out in lavender in front of everyone. He probably could have been accused of statutory rape. It was dangerous information to know.

A Request for Therapy

When I was in prison, I asked for therapy. I knew that if you closet a child abuser, all you get is a closeted child abuser. You are not curing him and you are making him twice as angry as he already is. He already has a low self-esteem and this denies him a chance to build himself up. I aggressively fought for therapy and was court ordered to go twice a week. The lieutenant was surprised by the court's response. So was I.

I went to SLAA once a week (Sex and Love Addicts Anonymous) and to a pastoral counseling center once a week. The SLAA meetings were an emotional reprieve from the prison. It was a place for help. It was a place where I could really feel some compassion and some understanding of what I was going through—

being sexually addicted to kids and having been sexually abused myself as a kid.

It did seem like an addiction to me. I was out of control. As an addiction, it started off small. It was like what others say about taking cocaine: you start taking one hit then you take two and three and four. I really had no control over it.

And I had no idea the addictive process was going on. It was amazing. It is so difficult for people to believe that. Sometimes it is so difficult for me to believe it too—to be a rational, educated human being and not to see that this was so horrible, abusive and betraying. That is what I pay for the most. People say you should have known it was that horrible. I should have known what I was doing to those kids. I should have known that this behavior had nothing to do with priestly life, or even being human. I did not know. I grew up in an emotionally deprived and sexually abusive environment.

The rejection I experience from friends and acquaintances is hard. People have not forgiven me for what I have done. People with whom I had healthy, intimate relationships for years reject me. They cannot deal with this reality. They just can't believe that I could do this and not know what I was doing.

There was a hideous poison that had gotten into my system. It had poisoned my life and now I was out poisoning other people's lives with no idea how horrifying it was. I feel like I want to escape from myself and jump into another person. I want to be somebody else because this truth in me is just devastating. It paralyzes me. *I did this.* I did it...great guy, great priest, lover of humanity. I did this.

I just cannot believe it. I cannot believe that I put myself in a predicament where it was going to cost me so dearly all my life. I am held in this state by society; I'm held here by myself. Though I am out of prison, I am still a prisoner.

I now know why I did it. I had been given permission to do it by an authority figure. "This was okay," he said, and nobody told me any different. That is the truth about victims becoming victimizers. There is no one outside that can peer in far enough into the victim's life to see something that is going on. It cannot be exposed. It was done in the dark. It was done in the darkness of my life.

I was about 12 or 13 at the time. The kids in my neighborhood had been getting together in little masturbation circles. I probably got involved in it heavier than anyone else. I was so emotionally deprived and hungry for some attention. My neighborhood friends liked sex with me. I felt connected with them. This is how I related to them and they to me.

The Scoutmaster was the pied piper of us all. He was a wonderful man. He knew a lot. He had a lot of experiences through the Korean War. He was great with his hands; he was artistic. He painted and did woodcraft and anything that a 12-year-old boy with a creative mind would love to get a hold of. I joined him.

He was the one who used to take me to concerts. I took him over to my house. He used to bring me to museums—art museums, science museums. At one time, I even wanted my mother to marry him.

He was a cultured person. I am an aesthetic person too. I just gravitated toward him and his interests. A lot of kids that I was friends with were his friends. I wanted to be with them and to be with him. So the relationship just grew in that way.

I have been thinking for weeks how it happened. When was the turning point? When did he put his hand on me and I said, "Okay, you can do this with me." I do not remember. I honestly do not remember. I guess I was so emotionally deprived and hungry for a man in my life I was not aware of what was happening. My father was gone and my mother was not in the picture. (She was always working.) When this guy showed interest in me, I went nuts. The relationship was very intoxicating.

We would go camping—a group of us (our average age was 16). Now, in retrospect, I can see a whole mess of things that were going on with him and the group. Now, in retrospect, I can see it. He used to feed us wine and we would go and have these lavish dinners at the parish Scout camp with lobsters and clams. He would fill us with wine. He was drunk himself and we were drunk, too.

I felt uncomfortable about the behavior, especially the physical abuse. I came home sore. My testicles hurt; my penis hurt; and my chest hurt because he had been on top of me. I felt I desperately needed his attention in my life at this time. I felt held, acknowledged, stroked and supported. That seemed more important than the pain.

My mother would not listen anyway. I knew I could not express my hurt to her because I experienced better attention from others who knew about love and care. We were a poor family. We separated from my Dad when I was ten years old. He had a lot of anger toward my mother so for years I was really scared of him. When my mother told me we were going to leave, I broke down and started crying. My mother said, "You can't cry like this. You've got to be the man of the house now."

Big Boys Don't Cry

That made me stand up as straight as a Marine. At that point I locked the door on my emotional stuff. I did not have permission to cry any more. I suddenly realized that I not only had to take care of myself; I had to take care of my mother, my brother and sister, too. Big boys don't cry.

I became my mother's counselor, her husband, her friend, her supporter, her analyzer, her protector. She is a very dependent woman. She puts on an air of independence but she is very dependent. I was responsible for her well-being. I became a "parentified child." With the little wisdom I had, I parented myself and the rest of the family.

It was tough. She had a horrible, horrible life, too. I still have a lot of resentment toward my grandmother. She allowed my mother to be sexually abused and to become pregnant not just once but twice by her alcoholic stepfather. Once I could see, but twice?!? Twice blew me out of the water. My mother had two children by him, one when she was 16 years old and another when she was 18. My mother put her stepfather in jail only because she saw him begin to go after her younger siblings. This dark family secret did not put me any closer to my grandmother, who is also my godmother.

This whole thing has been terribly systemic. To this day, most of my aunts and uncles are screwed up and so are most of their children. I do not know who my two half-sisters are. It was a surprise to me when I found out that in my last parish I was not more than two blocks down from where my mother had those two kids. At that point my mother's life came face to face with my own horror. My mother was a parentified child too. Sometimes I wonder if my uncle is not my mother's child. If he is, I would just lose my breath.

It is hard for me to want to go back into that crazy system. I cannot face their irrational stuff any more. The last time I went home, I had planned on seeing my mother alone. When I arrived, I found my grandmother sitting on the back porch. It was a surprise. Although she has been heartsick by this whole thing and I was her favorite grandchild, I never felt comfortable with her or liked being her favorite. I always felt as if something was going on in the background that I just did not quite understand.

In retrospect, I felt manipulated by her. I felt like she wanted a lot more out of me than I could give her. What she was after, I did not understand. Males in my family do not do well. They get sucked in by the women. They get manipulated. I had enough trouble being manipulated by my mother without being manipulated by my grandmother. When something great in my life happened, she'd say, "You don't deserve that." She just ripped me down any possible time and all was done "in jest." Everybody would laugh about it but I'd be crushed. She could not take anybody succeeding.

While my grandmother was on the porch, to be cordial I asked her how she was doing. After I came in, my mother said, "You are not being very nice to your grandmother." I said, "Ma, what do you want me to do? I asked her how she was and how she is doing." At that point I was thinking, "Ma, don't get me feeling kind of rough here. I'm having a hard enough time just being here." My mother said, "I don't understand why you feel so terribly toward your grandmother. She never did anything to you. She's loved you as the best one of the whole family."

Later on that afternoon, I told my grandmother, "Grandma, I am angry with you. I am angry about a lot of things that have happened to me that I can't understand and I just don't know what to do. I just don't know what to do with my relationship with you. I just don't know." Her only response was, "Don't get into trouble any more." She did not hear my pain; I left frustrated and weeping.

When I was in treatment, the Scoutmaster called me. He called me twice. He got the number from my mom; she did not know he was the perpetrator. Once my mother found out what he had done, she just about screamed. The first time he called he asked me how I was. That was before I knew that he was responsible for some of my behavior. He was partly responsible for where I was. I did not know that yet. I was just kind of shocked that he called me. I was glad he called. He meant an awful lot to me. The conversation was short. I was in a lot of pain with the issues I was dealing with.

The second time he called I was just beginning to discover that he may have been responsible for a lot of my behavior. I put that in the back of my mind when he called the second time. At that point, the issue of my victimization moved right to the forefront of my mind so I blasted him on the phone. He had no idea where I was coming from.

I asked him, "Are you still doing this?" "No," he said, "I quit because I am afraid of getting in trouble with the police." He had not told me the truth. He had not told me that this could get me in trouble with the police. So, at that point, I really got angry with him. "How many more have you done this with?" He said, "I have got an arm's length more of people behind you." I said, "Do you know how many lives you've destroyed? Do you know how many people are having trouble sexually because of you?" I feel so betrayed and ruined by his betrayal of my trust, my vulnerable trust. I trusted his wisdom and authority over me as a kid. I feel he poisoned my life.

Creating Family

When I was in the parish, I wanted to develop a lot of resources and connectedness with people, having them just love Christian life. I wanted them to love community life, to be helpful to one another and to have a genuine family. I think what I was doing was creating my family around me. I was trying to create the family that I did not have. And I did. I did it successfully.

People loved what I was doing because it was giving them what they needed. It was enabling them to express who they were, to develop their talents, and to really utilize themselves for the betterment of the community. They were doing remarkably well. I was doing remarkably well. I felt very appreciated and affirmed by them.

But, on the other side, there was a part of me that was extremely lonely. I did not feel good about myself. My relationship with my pastor was irritating. He was being manipulated by a woman—she practically told him when to go to the bathroom. She really irritated me. He did not have command of the parish. Everything was being filtered through her. If she said yes, he would do it. He had two priests sitting there who could have given him better counsel. What was going on really irritated me.

I was looking for a father figure, too. I was placing a lot of demands on him to be that father figure and I was not getting it. I was becoming more and more angry. While I was getting angry with him, I was overcompensating by doing these grandiose things in the parish, hoping to get his affirmation. Some of the things lasted, but the way they were done was not working out very well.

Going to Extremes

I was going to extremes. I was really angry and frustrated because I could not seem to get control of what was going on in my house and then I was going out doing all these grandiose things in the parish which were successful. But I was really burning, really extending myself. At the time, I did not feel like I was extending myself; I thought I was doing a good job.

"Jeez," I thought to myself, "these are powerful happenings here." On the other end, I was getting involved with kids who did not have a very stable emotional life...neither did I. One of the things that was going through my mind was, "I'm not going to allow what happened to me, as far as losing a father is concerned, to happen to these kids." I could see they were kids who were hurting and needed a father. I wanted to be that for them.

The needy and emotionally deprived kids received my attention the most. Since I was not relating well with my peers, I turned to parishioners and the kids for support. I know now that I identified with them. I identified with their needs and hurts. Theirs were the same as mine. And I parented them the same way I was taught.

Most of the kids were between 13 and 17 years old. There was only one 10 years old. I think what started it was I got involved with one of the kids who was sexually precocious. I was in the swimming pool and he just started all this sexual stuff in the pool. It tripped something; it pushed all my buttons. I got pretty sexually aggressive with him. It is one of the encounters that I can see in my mind and I feel so terrible about. I had no control and I was being very aggressive. Some months later, he wanted out....I could not stop.

I think he realized that he had turned on this fire in me and he did not know how to tell me to stop. I did not have enough wisdom or energy in me to know how to stop. We had sex. In retrospect, I can see it was a horrible scene. I think I did see a real fear in his eyes, a threat in his eyes, saying, "This is a bit too far out. I don't like this any more." He was 15 years old. I had a very strong relationship with his family.

I went to see a therapist because I had attempted to sexually assault a 17-year-old who told his parents. The therapist asked me if there had been any other occurrences of this going on and I said, "Yes." He said, "You're sitting on a neutron bomb." When he said that, I wanted to protect the kids. I did not want the kids I abused to be like me: a victim becoming a victimizer. I prayed to God on my way home that night to know what I should do. I asked God for the strength to visit each family and tell them what I was doing to their children.

I visited four families with my dreaded news and encouraged them to get their children into therapy. It was after the kids went into therapy that the state police got involved. This state has a mandatory reporting law and one of the therapists reported it.

I was charged with "abominable and detestable behavior against mankind," aggravated assault, and assault and battery. That really sounds terrible. It would be far from me to ever want to assault anybody. Little did I realize then that my behavior represented "assault." Now I do; it is revolting. I cannot think of assaulting anybody.

"Abominable and detestable crimes"—it sounds like you should have your carotid artery cut and you should be left to bleed on the streets. The state saw my actions as assault. I do not think the kids did...but perhaps the one who went home and told his parents did. My sexual involvement with their son gets very blurry to me. My life was a blur at the time. I was very depressed, very anxious. Things were just not going well in the parish. I was not doing well.

I was lonely, hurting and very angry. I was angry at the pastor. I was angry at the woman who manipulated him. I was angry at a lot of things. I never knew where it was coming from. In retrospect, I think I never got a fair shake in life. And no one wanted to hear that.

I did not know how morally wrong it was. My moral theology classes did not cover sexual abuse. But I did not like what was going on; I just did *not* like it. My life was a mess at the rectory. I was masturbating too much. Suddenly, my life was a mess with the boys. And I could not seem to get a hold of what was going on. I felt very confused, very alienated.

I have always had a good relationship with God. We always seemed to get through everything, but this was getting to be too much of an important issue. God did not seem to be buying my prayer. I would confess, repent and no sooner feel clean when I'd sin again. So I told God that I would give up my days off and work at the soup kitchen until he did something. I went to the soup kitchen with the mother of one of the kids I was victimizing.

"Victims Become Victimizers"

It was not more than three weeks later that I saw a television show called "20/20." It featured a young kid who had been sexually abused by his foster father and was in jail. He killed his foster father. Later on, we found out that his foster father had himself been sexually abused when he was a kid. The reporter turned and said, "Victims become victimizers." That was what broke my consciousness into reality.

It just hit me. Victims become victimizers. My heart raced. My mind whirled and my breathing became heavy. I knew I was a victim and now I was victimizing. I began to stop playing the victim and to accept the responsibility for my actions. I had become the victimizer. Regardless of who was at fault, I took hold of myself and said, "This is your responsibility." I did it.

Today, after much therapy, I have this image of a big black hole in my life that I was always trying to fill. I was trying to cap it off. Everything I threw in was hurting me more than it was helping. It was not until I decided to go around that hole and leave it alone that things started to get better. So now I do not try to fill that hole; I know it is there. I can feel it. It is a dark place to live; it is part of me.

But I know I cannot return to fill the hole because I know what is lost in there is so abysmal that it will never be replaced. So I do not try to fill the hole anymore. I build my life around it. Part of me will never be whole and that is the crippled part of me inside. That is my life. I have stopped living the lie and now live in the truth.

I am glad I have that image to hold on to. Any time I see a relationship or see a pattern of behavior beginning to develop that is not going to be beneficial, the black hole appears. The cover lifts and I realize that this is where I am headed. Some of the signs that I notice are when a relationship starts to get very abusive, sexually and controlwise. When I start feeling depressed and lonely and I start drinking, I begin to reflect and say, "No, this is not going to get you anywhere." When I am overworked and feel kind of anxious, I recognize that I need to start slowing down and to take things one at a time. I need to step back and pace myself. I say to myself, "Okay, you are getting kind of stressed out, kind of crazy."

One insightful book I read during recovery by M. Scott Peck, *People of the Lie,* had a powerful influence on me. He believes that we can be living a lie and we won't know it until someone shows us the truth. I was living in the lie of my family's denial and perpetrator's pathology. Peck says that unless we realize the truth is there, we cannot make a conscious decision to move out of the lie. Somehow the lie has affected our lives. And we need to take responsibility for all the damage that we have done and move on. That is what I am doing, taking responsibility for the damage that I have done, making sure this behavior never gets repeated in my life again, and moving on.

I wish people would believe that. I wish people would say, "He is okay; he understands himself; he's strong enough to hold himself together; he knows the resources he needs to get in touch to be sure this kind of behavior does not happen again." Church officials are especially worried that the church is going to be sued to the hilt or be embarrassed.

"I Lost My Integrity"

One of the most powerful lines I have read describes something that "plunders fortunes." This plunders fortunes. I have lost a lot. I lost a lot of my life. I lost the most important thing in life: I lost my integrity. I lost my home. I lost a lot of people whom I really loved and who meant a lot to me. I am glad I lost the people whom I was "sick" in love with; I am glad I lost them. I was in a lot of destructive relationships.

God has been faithful to me. I got angry with God, like Job, saying, "Why are you doing this to me?" One of the moral theologians talked about "ontic evil" in the world. I really got stuck in some strong ontic evil.

An important phrase from God stayed with me during this tragic time: *Deus est fides.* God is faithful. I felt God's faithfulness to me in these darkest hours, days, and years...and I still do today.

The church has been faithful, too, although I am somewhat estranged from the diocese. My bishop has remained faithful to me and I thank him for being so supportive throughout the entire process. However, I am not able to function as a priest in his diocese. I want to function as a priest again. There are some places that would probably take me. One bishop suggested a mission diocese far away. Is that where I will have to go? Another bishop heard of my situation and of my desire to return to ministry. His response was, "They cost us a lot of money." I am paying for it, and I want to stop paying.

So what does one do who cannot function as an active priest? The painful process is this: you try to get a job with an education that the "secular" world does not understand. You try to supplement it with an education you do not want. And you work at a job that you are uncomfortable with. In the beginning it was so frustrating, I had to muster all my energy and in a trance-like state go through my day, one hour at a time. But time moves on and there are other things to do.

I will turn 40 soon. During the birthday party, there will be about 60 people going through my new house. I am excited about it. Through this whole process I feel good about gaining some integrity with the people I am in relationships with. I thought I had lost my true character through this horror and disease. However, I am still the same warm, understanding person that I was before. It is showing through again. I am glad.

When asked to write this, I was grateful for the opportunity. I wanted to share my experiences with you and not hide them. Perhaps through this sharing God might send his healing grace to us all. I see this now as a priestly work. May it bring us healing.

An Adult Survivor
of Child Abuse Speaks

Anonymous

(Editor's Note: *The following account is by a priest and former client of the House of Affirmation. We thank him and his religious order for their generous help.*)

I don't remember much. Actually, I don't want to remember. It is not a conscious decision. Sometimes, I say to myself, "Listen, you need to look at this; you will feel a lot better if you do." But my insides resound with almost a scream, "No!" My therapist says that it is normal for an adult who was abused as a child not to remember—a type of amnesia. Well, I have definitely got amnesia.

When I went into therapy, I had no idea what was wrong. Things kept not working out right. I kept getting myself into crazy relationships with women. They would be the forceful and mothering types that would want to take care of me. They sensed I was in a lot of pain and were attracted by it, I think. They needed to soothe me. I needed to be soothed.

At first, it felt great. I thought, "Ahhhh, someone to make me feel better." But then I felt trapped and my anxiety skyrocketed. I wanted to get away but did not know how to get out. I felt powerless.

I did not understand what was going on inside me. It felt like a confused, jumbled mess. Actually, I lived most of my life this way and it seemed normal to me. But other people described me as "tormented," "isolated," or "driven." I must admit that I always felt tense and very much alone, but I just shrugged it off.

Finally, I really got myself into a mess. I was the pastor of a small parish. I was feeling lonely, tired and overworked. When Joyce offered to help me, I was so relieved. She wanted to help. She organized the rectory and changed the Mass schedule. She ran the parish picnic and oversaw the collections. She was a "take charge" type and she got things done. And she was there for me, too.

Things just slowly developed between us. I was in a lot of pain inside. I needed someone and she wanted to help. In the beginning, when she held me, I relaxed inside and the tension slipped away. My mind was filled with her and I could not think of anything else. Nothing else seemed to matter—she was going to protect me. I could not have stopped even if I wanted to.

At first, I was helping her—teaching her the ropes of parish ministry and how to do pastoral counseling. After a short while, you could tell there was a real chemistry between us. When she looked at me, it was as if she saw right into me. I knew it was nuts. I was risking everything: my parish, my reputation, my priesthood. Instead of backing off, the relationship was getting more and more intense. It felt great...at least in the beginning.

Some of the books I have been reading call it a "repetition compulsion." They would say that I was compulsively repeating aspects of an earlier abusive relationship in order to find some inner healing. It is like the woman who grew up in an alcoholic family who marries one alcoholic after the next. It seems crazy, but it was actually a misguided effort to repair the inner wounds, to master a situation that originally had been destructive. Unfortunately, such "repetition compulsions" are doomed to failure and only repeat the cycle of abuse.

"My Life Was Falling Apart"

I found out the hard way. My life was falling apart. Parishioners would have been blind not to know something was drastically wrong. I was so blind to what was happening that it never occurred to me that anyone would notice. Besides, what was there to notice? I told myself, "This is just a healthy friendship." Joyce and I spent an increasing amount of time together, and I spent less time in the parish. I could think of nothing else; I was obsessed. Other staff members even said something, but I wasn't really listening.

My first inkling that something was wrong was when I started feeling that I just wanted to "get away." I was feeling tense and anxious. I found myself more irritable and felt like I was out of control inside. I was becoming alienated from others and from myself.

The relationship between Joyce and me had changed as well. At first, I had been her mentor. After that, she took control of my life. She became an informal filter for people who wanted to see me. No one got into my office unless she approved it first. She said I was overworked and needed help. Actually, I did have a difficulty with boundaries, keeping people at a proper distance. It felt like everyone was all over me all of the time. My life was out of control and she promised to fix it. In the end, I felt smothered and controlled. My insides were screaming and I wanted to go far away.

I still had no real intention of changing anything because I really was not aware of how bad things were, despite what everyone was telling me. Finally, the parish staff confronted me and said that this had not been the first time I had such a relationship. They mentioned two others. Actually there were more. Always the same thing: an attractive, forceful woman takes an active interest in me. I feel protected and safe; she makes me feel warm and relaxed. But then it becomes too much; I feel threatened and want to run. But I cannot. I feel helpless and powerless. Then my anxiety rises and the whole situation blows up.

The superior of our order said I needed to go away for professional help. I was not happy to hear that but I went because he insisted. My therapist later told me that I was in pretty bad shape when I first came in. She said I was "decompensating"—a term that means I was falling apart. I sort of knew that. What I really did not know was how bad things were, how they got that way, and what could be done to bring health into my life.

It took me a long time to be comfortable with the therapist. I was not in the habit of opening my heart up to anyone, including myself. She said I looked tense. "Of course I'm tense." I said, "It is a tough world out there and there is a lot of pressure on me." What I did not know was that there was a great deal of internal pressure of which I was not consciously aware.

As the therapy progressed, I began to relax a little (not much!), just a little. Bits and pieces started to come back to me. They were like vague, forgotten images in a dense fog. I thought they were just the fantasies that everyone had but the odd thing was that they kept coming back, again and again, and they had a powerful effect on me.

In my mind I could see a hand reaching out toward me. I see the large fingers approaching and I sense that I am small. As the hand comes toward me, I begin to tense up. Every muscle tenses. I am powerless to stop the hand from coming. I cannot stop it and I want to scream!...But no sound comes out.

There is nothing I can do so I tense up, as if by making my muscles real tense I can keep the hand from touching me—or at least I won't really feel it. It is a horrible image, constantly haunting me. I cannot get rid of it. I feel tense and frightened everywhere I go.

I seem to be so vulnerable—in a negative sense. I cannot protect myself from anyone's advances. I cannot say, "No." I cannot drive a hard bargain. I feel exposed to everyone. How can I protect myself? I want to hide in a small room and close the door and lock it. In public, I prefer to sit in the corner with my back to the wall. I wish I had a gun to protect myself...but I sense it wouldn't fire anyway.

Other people look relaxed. They seem to have fun. They look like they feel safe. I do not begrudge them for it. I am happy for them. But I do not understand it. I do not know what "safe" feels like. I feel like I am tied up in knots. The image I like to use to describe how it feels is a rope; one of those thick ropes where each strand is twisted around the other until it forms a gnarled, knotted rope. I wish I could loosen it, but I cannot.

While I was in therapy, I had an important dream; that is where I first got the image of a rope. I dreamed that I was in a house and that upstairs everything was fine. People were laughing and enjoying themselves. But then I had an intuition that something was wrong in the basement. I went downstairs and there was a little boy with a rope around his neck. He was hanging by a noose made of the rope, but he was too light and small to hang to death. Instead, he was slowly choking and slowly dying.

For the first time I came face to face with how I felt inside—like a little boy with a noose around his neck who was slowly choking to death. Then my therapist asked me to do something which I thought was a bit unusual. She said, "Can you imagine yourself *being* the rope?" "This is nuts," I thought, "I am not the rope. I am the little boy in the dream." I tried anyway. As I felt what it was like to be the rope, I realized how much pressure and tenseness was a part of my life. I am that rope. God, I wish I could untie it.

People complain that I do not open up to them. They say that I am nervous and distant. Maybe so, but it feels a lot safer to me. I spend a lot of time alone; I feel better when I am alone. I would rather be alone than be abused, and those are the only two options that seem to exist for me. I get lonely sometimes and it hurts, but that is a pain I can stand. There are some pains I cannot stand....

The image of the hand continues to haunt me. Sometimes I imagine it actually touching me and, for a moment, it feels good. I am soothed and relaxed. Then I become sexually aroused and a feeling of guilt begins. There is something not quite right about this. And then the roof caves in. I get very upset and frightened and go out-of-control inside.

I learned that anything that makes you feel sensually good is wrong. You are guilty if you feel that touch. The way to minimize the hurt is to tense up, that is all you can do. The message is: "Don't relax; don't let down your guard because you know what will happen." I certainly do know what will happen, so I am constantly on guard.

"Maybe She Was Just Curious"

I do not think she really understood what she was doing to me. She was young, dark haired, and attractive—like all babysitters, I think. Maybe she was just curious. "What harm could come to such a little child? He is so young, he will never remember." I am not mad at her, I think, but if I had a gun (in my fantasy?), I would shoot her once in the head. It would be a clean shot and definitely fatal. Maybe that would stop the haunting images of the hand coming toward me. Children do remember.

She came to our house a lot. On the outside she seemed nice. She smiled and my mother liked her. My father had left my mother several years before. My mother would welcome her and I can remember wanting to scream: "She is not what you think she is. Don't let her in with me. Keep her away." But I was too small.

At first, I liked the attention she gave me. I was lonely. I did not know my father, and my mother spent her days and nights working. She did the best she could. How was she supposed to know what was going on? The babysitter paid attention to me; it felt good. No one ever touched me but her. I longed to have someone touch me.

But her touches confused me. It felt good but there were other feelings I was too young to understand. I was not able to understand our relationship. Babysitters are "big" people and they are supposed to protect "little" people. I was a little person. What she did didn't feel like protection. Do big people touch little people this way? I was confused.

There was something wicked in her eyes, I think. She looked at me with a glint of ravenous desire. If I painted a picture of my innermost image of her, it would be as a witch. Her fingers would be long, bony, and ugly. She would look at me as if I were a tasty morsel. She would want to devour me like the fairy-tale witch who wanted to eat Hansel and Gretel. When she came, I was devoured.

I won't let anyone touch me any more. I long for someone to hold me—to help me feel relaxed—but I cannot stand the touching. It is hard not to let people touch you. These days everyone wants to hug everyone else. They say, "You're not open if you do not hug" or "You just need to trust." I cannot. And when people force themselves on me, I feel abused all over again.

Some of the books I read say that abuse is often kept a secret and that the beginning of the healing process is to bring it out into the open as early as possible....How could I? At that time I was so young I knew barely enough words to say I was hungry or tired. It was impossible for me to communicate about something I did not understand and barely believed myself. Besides, the message I received from "big" people was: "These things are secret and powerful; we do not talk about them." And I was brought up to do what "big" people told me.

Somehow I knew that I was guilty. I felt like a dirty and disgusting little boy. In my head I knew that it was not my fault, but I could not convince my guts. My insides told me that I was part of it and that I got something from it. Is it my fault? It must be. Otherwise, why did it happen? I was good, wasn't I? If I was good why did this bad thing happen? I could only come to the conclusion that I must be bad.

Some books say that sexual abuse can seriously harm a child's future human relationships. Supposedly, the victim has a difficulty forming human bonds; the child may view others as potential abusers and the world as a hostile place....I do not feel that it has wrecked my future; the very concept of a future means nothing to me. Whenever I hear a priest talking about heaven, it seems like an empty concept. I cannot picture someone dying (i.e., going through a horrible experience) and then finding a place of peace and rest. I went through a horrible experience and now I am just hanging on.

I do not understand the idea of hope either. To me, hope means that something good will happen in the future. I think other people should have hope and I can see them experiencing good times. I cannot imagine such a good thing happening to me. I know that it seems crazy. My head says to my guts, "This is crazy. You are not different from everyone else. Good things have happened to you. Let go of all the garbage and have some hope." It does not work.

My therapist has encouraged me to have an inner dialogue between the "parent" and the "little boy" inside me. I have begun this inner dialogue. My parent says to the little boy inside, "So, what do you want? Why won't you relax and be happy?" The boy's response is clear, "I will not let go and relax until someone listens to me and hears my pain." My parent inside confesses it does not understand what the little boy with the rope around his neck is talking about. The boy says, "That is the problem! You really do not listen to the pain inside. You have no idea how badly I am hurting. You do not protect me."

My parents did not protect me. Dad was gone. Mother was working. They did not know. They did not know the secret until years later when the dark-haired lady was arrested. It is hard for a little boy to carry around such a big secret for so long. It was too hard for me.

God did not protect me, either. Why would God not protect a helpless little boy? It was not fair. Sometimes I like to read the Bible and imagine Jesus coming toward me. I try to put myself in the story and really experience a relationship with him. But if I am honest with myself, when Jesus comes close to me my reaction has become a bit distressing. Instead of welcoming and embracing him as I want to, I really would like to knock him down. I am mad at him and his Father. I do not like this feeling, but it is there.

Psychologists have a concept called an "introject." They say we introject the figures of our parents, that is, we take inside ourselves their personalities. These introjects then become part of our own psyches from which we often form our perception of God and ourselves. It is little wonder that we sometimes act like our fathers or mothers; we carry their image inside us. I have done this. Now, the unspoken conversation between the little abused boy and his unprotecting parents has become part of the inner dialogue in me.

I say to the boy, "I want to know. Tell me what happened." But the truth is, as the boy is quick to point out, I really do *not* want to know. It is too hard. It is too painful. I think I would explode if it came out or I might break down and sob uncontrollably—I do not think I could handle that either...so, it comes out slowly. Little pieces, bit by bit, come through the protective fog until I can see it for as long as I can stand.

Accepting the Reality of Abuse

My biggest struggle has been to accept the basic fact that I have been abused. I liked her. She was close to me; there was a bond between us, I think. The rest is only shadows in my dreams and vague images in a fog. They say that denial can perform a healthy function, particularly for a child. This denial can shelter the fragile psyche from more trauma than it can handle at the present time. But eventually the hurt, pain, rage and grief demand to be heard. They rattle around inside, causing all sorts of distressing symptoms, like my tension and crazy relationships, until they are acknowledged and worked with. I vacillate between admitting that I was abused and then dismissing the entire idea as pure fantasy.

But it must be true. I must have been sexually abused. When I deny it, life returns to being a confused, jumbled mess. Whenever I can say, "Yes, I have been abused," I feel better. Whenever I can accept another piece of the forgotten puzzle, I feel the rope untangle just a little. When I can listen to the sad, helpless, little boy with a horrible secret, life has a glimmer of hope. It is hard work. I have had to change a lot of ideas about myself and the world.

A breakthrough occurred when I was 42 years old and was on a retreat. I spent most of the weekend in prayer and silence as the retreat master had asked us. Halfway through, something powerful shot up from inside me. It was a strong voice that said, "I want to live!" I felt a real conviction that I wanted to live. As I reflected on that powerful voice I realized that for 42 years I had really wanted to die.

I never consciously entertained the idea of committing suicide. I was unaware of what I was really feeling inside. Rather, I did little things that would slowly kill myself. I drank too much; it made the pain stop a little—or at least numbed me to it. I took crazy chances on the highway when it was not really necessary. I always did the most dangerous thing possible. Who knows? Maybe the gods would smile on me and I would be killed.

Now, there is another voice inside. It is a powerful surge of energy that says it wants to live. I do want to live now, though truly living (and not slowly dying) is harder than it might sound. I have to face the pain. It is like someone has doused my whole body with gasoline and put a match to it. I am engulfed in pain, like a self-immolated Buddhist monk. Actually, the monk has it better—his pain is short lived.

Now I can hear the little boy in me scream and I feel sorry for him. Together we cry because it hurts so bad. Sometimes he gets mad and I listen to his rage....I will give him a voice now and let him speak to you:

> I am alone, unhappy, and in a lot of pain. No one listens to me—no one. Not even you. I have no one to help me and no one to protect me. I have had to fend for myself in a world that is too big and too powerful for me. I have become angry and resentful. I make your life miserable until you listen to me. All I really want is someone to listen. Someone to hold me in a warm and safe place. I need someone who will take care of me without hurting me. But it is hard for me to know if I can trust you so you have to be respectful of me and not push. I just want you to stay at a distance so I can see you and hear your voice. Slowly, I might learn to trust you. But do not ever touch me—I don't care how good your intentions are, please, do not touch me.

Signs of Hope

Initially, it was a hard message to hear. It was not what I thought I was like inside. But I knew it was right when I heard it. The mess inside is becoming a bit clearer. I am starting to understand myself.

The ironic thing is that the more I listen to the hurting and isolated child, the better I feel. The knot is slowly untwisting and there are moments when I feel downright free. I still have a long way to go, but I am now on the path to life. I am going in the right direction. There is hope in this.

My therapist is a sign of hope, too. She has been a warm and safe place for me. It was not always so. In the beginning, I had a hard time learning to feel safe—it was difficult for me just to be in the same room with her. I put her through hell, but she was patient. She encouraged me to tell her how unsafe I felt and to do anything I needed to do to feel safer. So I chose when we would meet. I chose how much space there would be between us (once I put her out in the hallway!). I even got to choose which room we would meet in; she had several. For a little boy who usually feels powerless, I felt empowered.

I am trying to be realistic about what the future holds. I still do not let my therapist or anyone else touch me. I will never be a totally relaxed person. People still complain that I do not open up to them enough. But it is better than before and they are learning to be patient. There are even a couple of priests in my life that I can truly call "friends." I still feel a special attraction (should I say compulsion?) to forceful women who understand my pain, but I recognize where it comes from and I let it go. I know what it will lead to and that will not help anyone.

I have been in therapy many months now. I am still mad at God, but I think that God can take it. I still imagine putting a bullet in the head of the babysitter, and I do not completely trust my therapist. But I do not see the hand much anymore and when it does appear, I just tell it to stop and it disappears. It cannot hurt me anymore. I still wish I could let someone touch me, but I do not think I ever will.

My superior has been supportive throughout and asked me to return to my parish. The people welcomed me as if I were a lost son who returned home. We wept together. It felt good. Joyce is in a different parish now and I have heard that she is happy. I am glad to hear news of her.

Last night I had a dream. I was being attacked by many strong and mean people. It was a war. But I defeated them and they were all captured. I went through their ranks and gave them back their weapons, but with no bullets. I felt compassion for them and a sense of bondedness. When I gave them their weapons back, it was an act of kindness: I thought they might want a souvenir of the war. And I remember thinking to myself and communicating to them, "It is over. The war is over. We are no longer enemies." I awoke with a sense of inner peace and, for a moment, I rested.

Psychological Intervention for Parishes Following Accusations of Child Sexual Abuse

Carroll Cradock, Ph.D.
Jill R. Gardner, Ph.D.

"Now I feel I can trust no one—not my husband, not my family, not the church. I no longer trust God."

These words, spoken by a parishioner whose pastor stood accused of sexual misconduct with a child, poignantly convey the psychological and spiritual crisis commonly provoked when allegations of child sexual abuse are made against a minister. Despite the demythologizing of the clergy that followed Vatican II and efforts to enlighten parishioners about the human vulnerability of their ministers, accusations that a clerical, religious, or lay minister has sexually abused children cause a profound sense of betrayal and shock.

Sister Patricia, Director of Religious Education for eight years at her parish, described her sense of anguish at learning that Father Bill had been arrested for molesting several junior high school boys during weekend religious retreats. Although Father Bill was free on bond pending trial, he had been admitted to a treatment center in a remote area before any of the parish staff or parishioners had had a chance to say goodbye. Sister Patricia struggled with intense and conflicting feelings: "I feel I should hate him for what he has done to this parish, but how can I? Father Bill was there for me when my father was dying. This man sat with me night after night in the hospital. He listened to me, he talked to me, he prayed with me. He was my rock of support."

Nancy, a third-grade teacher in her early 40s, wondered aloud about how her view of children and teaching had drastically changed after a male junior high school teacher was accused of molesting an eighth-grade girl. "I can't believe he would ever do anything like this," she thought. "You know how girls that age are. Somebody puts his arm on a girl's shoulder in a perfectly harmless way and her imagination works overtime. Nowadays you can't even give a first grader a hug without worrying about somebody saying you're a pervert. I never thought teaching would be like this."

Chuck, a truck driver and father of two sons, learned of the arrest of his pastor for aggravated sexual abuse when he turned on the evening news. Several days later, at a meeting held to provide support and guidance to parents during the ensuing crisis, Chuck expressed his deep sense of shame as he struggled to speak through angry tears: "My parents were married in this church and I was baptized here. I've lived here all my life and raised my kids here. When I saw my church on TV and heard my pastor was a child molester, I felt ashamed—more ashamed than I've ever felt in my life."

A Community-Wide Crisis

It is not only that a child is victimized; these accusations shock and demoralize the entire parish community. The psychological and spiritual crisis created by allegations of child sexual abuse extends to a broad range of people. The precipitating event for this community crisis usually takes the form of rumors of an investigation conducted by child protective officers, or an arrest accompanied by newspaper or television coverage. These events affect many different groups in the community, who then experience varying degrees of emotional upset. We refer to these groups as "target populations." They include victims and their parents, potential victims and parents, other children and parents, the perpetrator and his or her family, the parish, school and CCD staffs, parish leadership groups, and the wider parish community.

Members of these target groups present a variety of needs and issues. They may experience shock, a sense of betrayal, anxiety and/or anger at the church. Other needs and issues are more specific to one or another target population. For example, members of the parish team may feel guilty that they did not prevent the abuse. Similarly, in the case of a well-liked eighth-grade teacher who is accused but not yet brought to trial, the faculty may feel ambivalent about whether to allow the teacher to attend graduation ceremonies. Another issue arises for parish children whose revered pastor, teacher, or coach has been removed. They may feel confused, sad, and resentful over having to accept a substitute who is a stranger to them.

A variety of resources are potentially available to address the needs and issues of these target groups: diocesan liaisons, vicars and deans, diocesan consultants for education, youth ministers, Christian formation personnel, diocesan attorneys, parish staff, parish school staff, CCD teachers, consulting psychologists, local mental health service providers and lay leaders. Some of the target groups affected also function as resources to others, as represented schematically in Diagram 1. For example, an associate

Diagram 1

RESOURCES	TARGET POPULATIONS	
Diocesan CCD Liaisons	Parish Team	Victims/Parents
Diocesan School Office	School Staff	PotentialVictims/Parents
Diocesan Youth Ministry Office	CCD Staff	Other Children/Parents
Vicars and Deans	Parish Leadership	Perpetrator/Family
Diocesan Attorneys		Wider Parish Community
Psychological Consultants		
Providers of Mental Health Services		

pastor, although shocked and traumatized to learn that his pastor may have abused children, is one of those persons most likely to provide emotional support and spiritual guidance to traumatized

parishioners during the weeks and months following the allegations.

These various resource people provide or facilitate interventions, which may assume a wide range of formats. There might be
consultations, one-to-one meetings or psychological assessment,
verbal or written educational materials, or meetings of staff, parents, children, or the whole community. Whether the format entails individual or group meetings, written materials, or counseling sessions, the goal of these interventions is to assist all those
affected to absorb the shock and doubts created by the allegations, face their feelings, and restore their capacity to place their
confidence in others.

The relationship of the components of the situation described
above is summarized in Diagram 2. In brief, the precipitating

Diagram 2

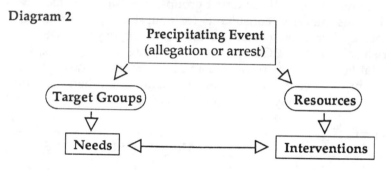

event (an allegation and/or arrest) creates target groups who
have needs and issues, while also mobilizing resources which can
provide interventions. The interventions are brought to bear on
the needs; the needs determine the interventions. The goal is to facilitate adaptation to the event. The interventions provided
should be based on a familiarity with the impact of these allegations on adults and on children in general, as well as on specific
target groups in particular. We turn now to a brief summary of
common adult and child reactions.

Adult Reactions
We conduct our lives on the basis of certain implicit assumptions.
These include the belief that events are orderly, the world makes
sense, and there are certain things one can count on. We also
believe that we can protect our children and keep them safe, espe-

cially when we entrust them to the church. Charges of child sexual abuse by a member of the parish community are unexpected, unnatural, and startling events that violate our sense of order, faith, and trust. Such assaults on basic assumptions are always traumatic. The accusations lead people to read and hear terrible things about someone who, more often than not, is a valued member of the school or parish community, appreciated for his or her devotion and service, well-liked by children, and respected by adults. People are left confused, not knowing what to make of this.

Emotional Reactions

In response to this assault on basic assumptions, parishioners experience a sense of shock, denial, disbelief, anxiety, and betrayal. Sometimes parents blame themselves: "I should have known or seen; I should have been more involved, more careful." Their failure to protect the children leaves such people feeling guilty, ashamed, and inadequate. Both self-esteem and self-confidence are diminished.

Alternatively, people may point the finger of blame outward: "The church should have known, or the school, or the police. They should have prevented it." The failure of these groups to have done so leaves people feeling angry, resentful, and betrayed.

When there is coverage of the events in the public media, parishioners feel exposed, embarrassed, exploited, enraged, and hurt. They easily feel that the reputation of the parish is tarnished, and may experience a sense of shame about their own membership in the parish when talking to outsiders.

In a situation that creates as many different and often conflicting feelings as this one does, it is typical for people to have different reactions at different points in time. This can be confusing to others who are going through their own set of reactions, possibly in a different sequence. Within a single family, for example, the wife may be feeling worried, while the husband is feeling enraged and the child is feeling embarrassed. At another moment, they may all have switched to a different set of feelings, creating many opportunities for tension and misunderstanding.

It is also natural for certain stressful events to trigger old feelings from earlier events. For example, people with early experiences of a traumatic betrayal of trust may re-experience some of the pain, anguish, and disillusionment they felt at that time. Similarly, those who have been sexually exploited as children may find old memories and feelings also suddenly re-emerging. Realizing this helps clarify people's intense reactions to these events.

Religious Crises

Evidence that such a grave betrayal of trust has come from within the parish staff is experienced by parishioners as an assault on such traditional images of the church as City of God, Light of the World, God's representative on earth, and sanctuary from harm. Moreover, to many Christians, events such as these test their faith in divine providence. Accustomed to turning to the church for comfort and guidance in coping with life's adversities, parishioners may feel abandoned and confused when the threat comes from within the church. Feelings of betrayal can provoke a crisis of faith, particularly when the alleged abuser is a priest or a member of a religious congregation. Some people may feel that if they cannot trust God's representative, they are abandoned by God.

Behavioral Reactions

Stressful events create changes not only in how we feel, but also in how we act. People commonly suffer from physical problems, such as headaches, stomachaches, and insomnia. Others may experience nightmares. Parishioners may have more difficulty than usual concentrating, finding themselves preoccupied or dwelling on the events. They also may become more tense and irritable, overreacting to minor provocations and arguing more with family members or co-workers.

How stressful a given individual will find these events depends in part on how everything else is going in that person's life. People who are already struggling with serious medical, personal or financial problems have fewer internal reserves with which to absorb the shocks of these events.

Issues and Questions

Whatever their particular emotional and behavioral reactions, parishioners invariably are flooded with a series of questions and concerns. They want to know, and yet fear knowing, the full impact of the abuse on the victims' emotional and sexual adjustment. They wonder how damaged the children are or might become later, and worry about whether they will "get over it" and be "normal." Because this is unfamiliar territory, they feel ill-prepared to help their children with it. Parents wonder how to raise the subject and how to respond to their children's feelings and reactions.

Psychological Help

One of the most immediate tasks parents of actual victims face is securing psychological help for their children. Financial concerns, lack of familiarity with mental health services, and conscious and unconscious fears that yet another adult (i.e., the therapist) may exploit their children are all dilemmas faced by these parents.

The Legal System

The legal system presents another set of issues and questions. Public allegations usually involve a single child or a small number of children. Because many pedophiles have multiple victims, however, questions arise as to whether other children have remained silent about the abuse.

Embarrassment, loyalty, or fear of retaliation can all prompt children to remain silent. Parents usually feel ill at ease about broaching the subject with their children, not only because this is an unfamiliar and sensitive topic, but also because they may be afraid of what they will learn. Nevertheless, public authorities, i.e., police and child protective organizations, often want to interview other children in order to identify additional victims. In some states, parents may decide whether to allow their children to undergo interviews by police and child welfare officials, while in other states they do not have a choice.

When children are interviewed, they often must speak to investigators not once, but several times, a process which may aggravate the trauma. Confronting the perpetrator in court and undergoing cross-examination are steps that may be either restorative or debilitating for the child, depending on the circumstances. Since most parents are unfamiliar with these procedures, they need access to consultants who can provide information as they make these hard decisions about their children's participation in the legal process.

Mixed Feelings and Divided Loyalties

Feelings about having known about the abuse, or not, and having told, or not, also create a series of concerns: anxiety about having acted; guilt about not having acted; or anger about having tried to act and feeling that "no one listened." People who have come forth with information may wonder about the impact of their behavior on the alleged perpetrator and share a sense of responsibility for his or her fate, or worry about the impact of their behavior on the parish. Reactions of peers, family, teachers, and friends are another source of potential problems. Youngsters who are reluctant to believe the accusations may scapegoat those who made them, hurling blame against the accuser rather than the accused for bringing trouble to the parish.

Divided loyalties run high in situations of alleged sexual abuse, in part because the person accused is usually well-known and liked by many people in the parish. The divided loyalties may be not only toward the perpetrator, but also toward the school and parish staff. Close affiliation and friendship with the alleged perpetrators in the past leads many people to feel concerned about their well being and their fate.

After the initial shock, some may continue to doubt that the allegations are true and insist that at the trial "the truth" will inevitably emerge, vindicating the accused. Others may just as strongly maintain that the accused is guilty. These opposite opinions can polarize a parish. Regardless of opinions about the truth of the allegations, anger and embarrassment at news media coverage is the norm. Parish members complain that they feel violated and "raped" by television reports and sensational newspaper coverage.

Among parish, school, and CCD staffs, feelings of shock, betrayal, guilt, loss, anger, and responsibility are often intensified because of their closer working relationship with the perpetrator, toward whom they may now be ambivalent. Feelings of compassion and pity alternate with feelings of rage at the accused for exploiting children whom they know and care for. Co-workers themselves may be strongly divided regarding the guilt or innocence of the accused.

Members of the parish staff move to the center of parish attention as they deal with reactions and needs of parishioners, parents, children, and each other. They must attend not only to the allegations themselves but also to the official parish response, including the hiring of replacement workers for the accused and public statements made about the perpetrator and victim.

Confidentiality
Confidentiality creates yet another set of problems for the parish

staff, who may know more than they can share publicly at any given moment. This leaves parish staff vulnerable to attack for not responding as parishioners expect them to. They may be accused of indifference or "covering up." Parish staff, therefore, invariably need assistance regarding what they can share with whom and how to deal with the many questions that are put to them by parents, children, and parishioners in general.

In cases where the accused is a priest, all those who have been ministered to are touched by the allegations. It is not uncommon for these parishioners to feel betrayed not only by the accused, but by God for allowing this to happen. The incomprehensible accusation that a priest, "another Christ," may have sexually abused children leads some people to suspect that he may have been an impostor. This may be expressed in doubts that the marriages, baptisms, or confessions conducted by the accused were valid sacraments.

For all adults in the community, there is increased anxiety about the safety of children in general. People become concerned with knowing whom to trust, whether there was earlier, undisclosed abuse, and how to protect children from being molested in the future. Parish staff usually confront angry parishioners who demand to know how staff and volunteers are screened and supervised.

While children naturally become the prime focus of concern and intervention when allegations of child sexual abuse rock a parish, it is important to recognize that the adults have their own intense reactions to these deeply upsetting events. The concerns of the adults often must be addressed before they are able to intervene effectively on behalf of the children of the parish.

Child and Adolescent Reactions

Regardless of age, the major psychological effects of these allegations on youngsters are a sense of betrayal and sexual anxiety. In order to survive and develop, children must rely on adults to protect and care for them. When any known, well-liked, and trusted adult (as most perpetrators are) is accused of pedophilia, children feel at risk of harm not only from that person, but from all trusted adults who care for them. Sexual anxiety is elicited in many children because they are faced with the fact that even a familiar, reliable adult has failed to handle his or her sexuality in a mature, healthy manner. Because these children, as well as adolescents, are still in the process of sexual maturation, this awareness of adult sexual deviance can produce anxiety regarding their own capacity to integrate and express sexual impulses as their development proceeds. In addition to these two generally expected reactions, other factors will determine the impact of these events on children and adolescents.

What the Child Brings to the Event

The first factors that must be considered are the child's history and present circumstances. Allegations of sexual abuse are heard by a child of a specific age from a particular family which holds certain beliefs and attitudes. This boy or girl has a unique psychological makeup (temperament, developmental stage, emotional stability) and relationship to the accused. Moreover, some time ago he or she may have tried to alert adults about the abuse. These aspects of each individual, as well as his or her prior experiences with traumatic betrayal, sexuality, and any current sources of stress, all combine to influence how he or she will feel, think and behave as the words of the allegations register.

Obviously, the shock of a 6-year-old may be expressed in a far more overt way than that of an adolescent who assumes an air of cynicism and indifference. Similarly, a highly emotional child will be likely to respond with more intensity than will a less responsive one. Some children will have fewer resources to sustain them. Most vulnerable are those children who are already feeling fragile, either because their psychological development has been troubled or because they are currently facing other stressful realities, such as family arguments, peer conflicts, or academic problems. These children are likely to need more help in order to cope with the emotional upheaval and disruption in their daily lives.

In regard to the psychological importance of the offender, it is likely that, because pedophiles are usually attractive and helpful to children, many will have experienced the alleged offender as a revered and idealized friend. These youngsters are likely to be more shaken by the allegations than are those who maintained a more distant and neutral relationship.

Recent figures estimate that approximately one-third of girls and at least half as many boys are sexually abused by someone before age 18 (Finkelhor, 1979; Russell, 1983). Consequently, it is to be expected that in any given parish, a substantial number of children have been sexually victimized by a family member or by someone else. Among this group of abused children, the allegations will stir up powerful feelings which can be expressed in a variety of ways. Even if a child has not been sexually abused, but has experienced a strong sense of betrayal of trust by an adult, these events may further erode that child's confidence in the adult world. It is not uncommon for children to feel they tried to tell their parents or teachers that something was awry. Typically, their attempts are now forgotten by adults or recalled as tentative or vague. Nevertheless, when public allegations are made, these boys and girls feel angry that "no one listened."

What the Event Brings to the Child

A second set of factors that governs children's reactions revolves around the accusations themselves and their consequences. Those who were sexually abused face profoundly painful thoughts and feelings. They almost always require some mental health services. In regard to non-victims, generally the most traumatic effects occur under the following circumstances: strong identification of the child with the victim or victims; allegations of greater rather than lesser deviance; strong feelings of responsibility for prior secrecy and/or disclosure; extensive publicity; considerable upheaval in routines and relationships; and the continuing presence of the perpetrator in the parish or neighborhood.

Most perpetrators are alleged to have molested only boys or only girls. Those of the same sex as the victim will feel more intense anxiety than will the others. Any child who has taken an active role in disclosing the abuse can be expected to feel a greater degree of responsibility for the fate of the perpetrator as well as for the emotional trauma he or she, and others, now feel. Some children may wonder if they might not have done better to remain silent.

In addition to the allegations, many other changes occur in children's lives. Usually the accused is removed from the parish team or faculty and may disappear altogether. The boys and girls must then face the loss of a familiar and well-liked figure and adjust to a "stranger" substitute. This adds to the sense of disruption in their daily lives. News media coverage can aggravate the situation for children, depriving them of the privacy they need to cope with these stressful events and leaving them feeling embarrassed that a "pervert" was at their school or parish. Guilt by association may prompt them to refuse to wear school or athletic uniforms or other clothing which associates them with the parish and school.

In addition to coping with their own feelings, children must live with the reactions of their parents. Parents and other adults often pressure them, consciously or unconsciously, to decide whether the accused is innocent or guilty or to adopt the parents' feelings toward the perpetrator. Moreover, children sometimes place additional pressures on each other: they may blame any child who disclosed the abuse, as well as scapegoat the actual victims.

In some cases, the accused may be released on bond, pending trial. He or she may then remain visible in the community at shopping areas or Sunday Mass. When this happens, the children's anxiety dramatically increases as they continue to feel a sense of fear and danger for themselves and the perpetrator. The fact that the accused is at liberty can also provoke a sense of confusion and outrage at the judicial system.

Psychological Reactions of Children and Adolescents

The many reactions of children and adolescents are highly variable from day to day: denial, anxiety, anger, guilt, confusion, and concerns about sexuality are all to be expected.

Denial   This is usually the first reaction. For children, it is usually impossible to integrate the idea that a seemingly good person did something bad to children. They may resolve this dilemma by denying one part of the allegation or another, e.g., "It's a lie; he didn't do it," or "He wasn't a priest (teacher); he was a fake, an impostor."

Anxiety   The shocking and unexpected nature of these events is a signal to youngsters that their assumptions about the apparent benevolence of adults they trust are flawed. This rift in their presuppositions may lead them to worry that still other adults in their lives may hurt them or that other calamities will happen, e.g., car accidents or illnesses of parents. This anxiety may express itself in jumpiness, fears, nightmares, concentration problems and avoidance of persons, places, and activities associated with the perpetrator.

Anger   The anger may arise from several issues: the sense of betrayal of trust by the perpetrator; anger that other adults could not or did not prevent it; being forced to face the sexuality of adults prematurely; exposure in the media; and changes in their daily routine. The way the anger is expressed depends on the youngster's age. Very young children tend to be overly oppositional and to have more tantrums, while adolescents show cynical, provocative behavior toward each other and adults.

Guilt   Depending on their degree of involvement in the alleged abuse, particular children may feel guilty for different reasons. Those who have not been abused may feel guilty that they emerged unscathed from their contacts with the perpetrator. Those who participated in the disclosure tend to feel responsible not only for the fate of the perpetrator, but also for the consequent disruption in many people's lives, e.g., the loss of the perpetrator, the hiring of new teachers or coaches, news coverage which followed from the disclosure. These guilt feelings may find their expression in an increase in prayer, depression, self-sacrificing deeds, ruminations, blaming of others, or accidents and other potentially injurious behavior.

Concerns About Sexuality   The allegations force an awareness in youngsters that sexuality can be dangerous and that known, apparently benevolent adults can lose control of sexual impulses. Their anxiety may be heightened since sexual exploration is common, particularly among adolescents. They may now worry that whatever sexual activity they have engaged in which they thought was questionable may be a sure sign that they, too, could "become a pervert." The overt expression of sexual anxiety in these circumstances usually takes one of two forms: withdrawal or hypersexuality. Some adolescents may adopt or increase ascetical and religious practices and express puritanical attitudes. Others may increase sexual language and activities or dress more provocatively.

Confusion   It is usually not comprehensible to children how someone "good" could do something so bad. In addition, they are confused about how an adult could want sex with a child. Besides these perplexing questions, children and adolescents are usually quite unfamiliar with the judicial system. Upon learning how it works, they may become even more confused and angered by the length of time until guilt or innocence is decided and punishment is levied.

A Model for Intervention

We have indicated in the previous sections that allegations of child sexual abuse affect the whole parish community, creating psychological trauma and vulnerability in many different forms. In the face of these events, it is important to intervene, and to do so actively and quickly. But for those whose task it is to help a parish deal with such allegations, the problem can feel a bit like an eel that constantly darts away just as they are about to grab it. As the description of reactions provided above illustrates, in any given situation there are multiple issues, needs, and possibilities for intervention.

What workers need in order to deal effectively with this task is a way to organize their thinking about the situation as a whole. A good starting point is the identification of relevant target groups and their needs, as well as potential resources and interventions.

This still leaves the question, however, of how to decide both what to do and how to do it. While each situation is unique, we have found that there are certain general principles for making decisions that transcend the specifics of any given situation. These can serve as a guide for both planning and evaluating any program of action.

General Principles

1. *The church must take the initiative in this situation, in reaching out to, rather than retreating from, the members of the parish community.* The importance of timely psychological and pastoral intervention cannot be overemphasized. In any kind of emotional crisis, people are highly responsive to those who first appear to offer assistance, and to those who fail to do so. The events under discussion here threaten people's very connection to their church, their faith, and their God. If the church falls into a defensive or reactive position, that connection is at greater risk of being severed. When the blow comes from within the church, then active outreach from that source is more necessary than ever in order to heal the wounds.

2. *Forums must be established in which relevant groups of parishioners can air their fears and concerns and obtain the information they need.* In addition to providing information, such forums reduce anxiety, create opportunities for people to express their feelings and regain a sense of calm, and facilitate problem solving. The forum might be a community meeting, a parent-teacher conference, a conversation with the pastor, or a letter inviting parents to contact teachers if they have questions.

3. *It is always best to use the parish's natural networks and leadership, with other professionals providing consultation, education, guidance, and support as needed.* Teachers, for example, are usually in a

better position to talk with their students than are consultants from the school office. Similarly, parents are in a much better position to talk with their children than is anyone else, including experts in child psychology and sexual abuse. The consultants might be very helpful to parents and teachers, however, in providing information that will help them feel more prepared to take on the task of helping the children work through their feelings. Similarly, the pastor is often in the best position to reach out to affected families, and to provide leadership over interventions in the parish in general. However, he, too, might benefit greatly from consultation with others who have dealt with situations like this before. The general principle is to promote self-help within the parish, using consultants to help the natural leaders and caregivers increase their sense of comfort, confidence and competence to deal with the situation.

An assessment of the natural networks within the parish, including both strengths and needs, helps to determine appropriate roles. Whether, for example, it is the parish school principal or the pastor who might best deal with a group of faculty, or a particular family, is something that will vary from parish to parish. This kind of assessment is needed to formulate action plans (see below) and to determine what outside resources might be needed.

Diocesan Liaisons

Because of the intensity of emotion, the complexity of the psychological and legal issues involved, and their unfamiliarity with such events, most parishes find it very difficult to deal with the fallout from allegations of child sexual abuse without help from outside the parish. *We strongly advocate the use of diocesan-level facilitators or resources.*

Diocesan-level liaisons are a source of information and support. They may become a vehicle for pulling parish leadership together and can help in several other tasks: assessing the strengths and needs of staff, educating helpers within the parish and school staff, and formulating a plan of action. Diocesan people are often in a better position to clarify and mobilize educational, legal, and psychological resources. They assure continuity, coordination, and integration of interventions, as well as follow-up. Most important, they bring the experience of other parishes which have faced similar problems.

Action Plan

Because problems can mushroom rapidly, it is essential to organize quickly the interventions made in a parish following accusations of child sexual abuse. Action plans can be described both in
terms of their methods and their components.

The method for devising an action plan involves three steps: 1)
assessing the target groups and needs; 2) determining resources
and interventions; and 3) assigning roles and a timetable. Who are
the vulnerable individuals and groups? What problems are anticipated? Who is in the best position to deal with each? What context or setting would be most effective for doing so? In what order
should the steps be taken and when? These are the kind of questions that will lead to a systematic plan of action.

The components of the action plan can also be described in a
way that cuts across specific situations. First, the plan must include a way to provide and coordinate information in an ongoing
way. Second, it needs to create forums for fears, concerns, and/or
problem solving. The plan should promote self-help and mutual
support within the parish community, while also providing linkage to appropriate resources both within and outside the parish,
particularly educational and psychological resources. Third, sensitive integration of concerns of parishioners in the regular liturgi-
cal events of the parish is important, as people often want to pray
about this crisis. Finally, the plan should assure the stability and
maintenance of parish and school routines during this difficult
time.

Whatever the specific plan of action in a given parish, there are
certain common principles about what helps adults and children
cope with the problems that have been described.

Helping Adults

1. *Helpers try to convey that the feelings and reactions people show are
normal, legitimate, and expected responses to what has occurred.* In order to promote self-acceptance, it is important to normalize feelings and reactions. People's reactions express the psychological
meaning of those events, and as such are neither good nor bad,
right nor wrong. Whatever a person feels is appropriate; the first
step in managing such feelings is being able to accept them.

2. *People need information and education.* For example, guidance
about how to talk with the children, or what to expect from the investigative bodies and legal system is extremely helpful. Such in-

formation makes people feel more competent and therefore less overwhelmed and anxious. Educational interventions also help with the process of normalizing reactions and self-acceptance.

3. *Parishioners may want to pray about their concerns.* Scripture readings, homilies, and Prayers of the Faithful all provide opportunities to alleviate feelings of abandonment and integrate the crisis in the shared prayer life of the parish.

4. *Returning to "business as usual" as much and as quickly as possible is also therapeutic.* Re-establishing family, school and parish routines helps to restore parishioners' damaged sense of order. It helps make things predictable again, restoring a modicum of people's faith, as well as their confidence in themselves and the world around them.

Re-establishing routines should not be confused with putting the events out of one's mind. The value of talking and listening, at all levels, cannot be overemphasized. Expressing feelings promotes healing; letting them build inside does not. Listening to others is also therapeutic, particularly when people can listen without criticism or argument. An accepting, nonjudgmental response to the outpourings of others is one of the most effective ways to help people come to terms with their own feelings.

Sometimes either the timing or personal meaning of these events is such that it triggers more than someone can comfortably manage using only the support offered by the family and the parish. The more intensive forum provided by one-to-one counseling with a trained mental health professional may be useful in those cases.

Normalizing reactions, providing information and education, stressing the value of talking and listening, re-establishing disrupted routines, and linking people to mental health resources when needed are all ways that people working in the parish can help adults cope with the trauma created by the allegations and/or arrest.

Helping Children

The recovery process from the assault on children's trust in the adult world is a slow one, which may take weeks or months, depending on how severely a child's trust has been damaged. After the initial days of shock, confusion and intense feeling, the recovery process is often quiet, punctuated by unexpected questions, reactions and disruptive or withdrawn behavior. During this phase, youngsters' preoccupation with the thoughts and feelings triggered by the allegations or abuse waxes and wanes. Reactivation of the original trauma usually coincides with the publicity surrounding such legal proceedings as continuances, trials, or sentencing.

1. *Essential to the recovery process for children and adolescents is the provision of an empathic, steady "holding environment" by the adults who care for them.* This psychological "holding environment" provides the structure and support which enables children to absorb the reality of the trauma, tolerate the emotional upheaval, and slowly restore their faith in the adult world and themselves. Not surprisingly, children are helped by many of the same things that help adults: normalizing reactions, information, being listened to with acceptance, and the re-establishment of disrupted routines. Because they are the adults on whom a child must depend, parents, teachers and ministers are in a position to help children in ways that transcend what any child psychologist could do.

2. *In almost all cases, it is best if the parents are the first to raise the issue of allegations.* Foremost among the ways to help is the adults' willingness to bring up the issue of the allegations to the child. Parents, when faced with this task, often feel helpless: "I don't know what to say...I'm too upset to talk about it." Consultation with resource people is usually effective in helping parents decide upon a time and manner of inviting children to share their feelings about what has happened.

Having made it clear they are willing to talk, parents should then respect the child's wishes about talking immediately or at a later time. The willingness of adults to "go at a child's pace" in discussing such painful events reassures children. Young children, for example, may make one comment, e.g.,"I hate him" or "I miss him," and then ask to go out to play. Statements from adults that their feelings, thoughts and questions are normal facilitate acceptance of reality and restore self-esteem.

Patient tolerance for repeated questions helps children. It is common for them to ask the same questions many times, even months later, despite having been given a complete explanation. Anxiety and confusion prompt these repeated questions; hearing the explanation repeated provides a calming effect. The repetition soothes children.

Opportunities to convey their feelings to the alleged perpetrator can help children in situations where the accused has disappeared from the parish or school. Some children ask to send letters or cards to the person and feel better when they are assured that the principal or pastor will see that they are delivered.

3. *It is critical that parents speak honestly and neither lie nor evade issues the children raise.* Two things are essential to rebuilding trust in adults: honesty from adults, and promises kept by adults. Each honest statement begins to restore trust. When faced with questions of fact or motivation they cannot answer, it is best if parents simply explain that they do not know. Typical questions are: "Why did he do that?" "Will he go to jail?" An adult response such as "I don't know. . . I wish I understood all this better myself" can actually soothe children's anxieties and provide hope because it conveys that adults can go on in the face of confusing and disturbing events.

Keeping promises is always important in raising children, but it takes on heightened meaning during the recovery process. Each promise kept is a sign to children that even though they were betrayed by one adult, the adult world is still generally trustworthy.

In the weeks and months that follow the disclosure, episodes of emotional turmoil and atypical behavior are to be expected. Adult sensitivity to the meaning of these episodes is another component of the "holding environment" needed for recovery. Sensitivity, however, is not to be mistaken for permissiveness or lack of limits. Now, more than ever, children need the sense of security created by consistent, familiar routines at home and school.

With time and adult support, most children re-establish a "wiser" but genuine sense of trust and security. For some children, however, this will not be sufficient. These children will continue to display signs of distress and/or behavioral problems. Linkage to mental health professionals skilled in treating child sexual abuse can help these children re-establish their equilibrium. Children who are victims of sexual abuse should always be evaluated by a psychiatrist, psychologist or clinical social worker who specializes in the assessment and treatment of these problems. The parish team or faculty can help by providing parents with referrals to such specialists.

By recognizing that recovery is a process, providing a steady environment, allowing reactions to occur, talking and listening to feelings, being honest, keeping promises, maintaining normal routines, and monitoring for symptoms, adults in the parish community can effectively respond to the needs which the parish's children will manifest in reaction to allegations of sexual abuse.

Conclusion

As we have emphasized throughout, allegations of child sexual abuse by a member of the church shake a parish to its very core, creating a crisis for the entire community. People start out feeling shocked and bewildered by the news itself, as well as over-whelmed and helpless about how to respond to the myriad problems the event creates. They are presented with a situation they never imagined having to deal with, or, perhaps, with their worst fears come true.

Despite the complexity and severity of these problems, we believe that tremendous healing power resides within the parish community. With appropriate leadership, education, and use of outside resources, that power can be mobilized in such a way that both staff and parishioners can effectively respond to the needs of the community. Immediate, active intervention serves not only to heal emotional wounds, but to restore parishioners' faith in their church, in each other, and in themselves.

References

Finkelhor, D. *Sexually Victimized Children.* New York: Free Press, 1979.

Russell, D. (1983). Incidence and Prevalence of Intrafamilial and Extrafamilial Sexual Abuse of Female Children. *Journal of Child Abuse and Neglect,* 7, 1983, 133–139.

Officially Responding
to an Accusation of Sexual Abuse:
Reflections of a
Diocesan Communications Director

Carol Stanton

A Hypothetical Scenario
Late Thursday Afternoon The chancellor is trying to clear the mail on his desk and escape. Tomorrow is his day off. This weekend he is covering for one of the priests in an outlying parish. His telephone rings. On the other end is a very distraught man who says his 12-year-old son told him he had been fondled by the parish priest, not once but many times, at altar boy camp-outs, and even in the sacristy. He is demanding that the bishop do something about it immediately.

The chancellor asks the man to keep this quiet. He promises to get to the bishop and get right back to the man. Privately, the chancellor is thinking, "I know this priest. I cannot imagine that he would do anything like this. The man sounds like a trouble-maker. That parish is known for its rabble-rousers. He is probably overreacting. I will call the priest."

The chancellor puts a call in to the priest only to find that it is his day off. The chancellor leaves a message with the parish volunteer. She has trouble understanding who the chancellor is and she asks him to spell his name. He hangs up, thinking, "I won't bother the bishop with this until I have more facts. This could be nothing." He makes a mental note to call the priest from home that evening. He calls this boy's father back and says he is working on this case and that he will call him first thing in the morning. The chancellor finishes his mail and leaves the office.

That evening he gets word that his father is gravely ill. He asks a priest friend to cover his weekend work and he immediately flies home.

Friday 10:30 A.M.
The chancery switchboard takes a call for the chancellor. The operator explains that the chancellor will be out all day. The caller insists on getting in touch with him but the operator explains that it is the chancellor's day off and there is no way to reach him. The caller gets angry and insists on speaking with the bishop. The switchboard transfers the call to the bishop's secretary. She explains that the bishop is out of town until Monday. The caller grows more irate. He tells her that this is a delicate situation involving his young son and the behavior of his parish priest. The secretary says she cannot pass this situation on to anyone else— only the chancellor can handle it. The man leaves his number and tells her to contact someone who will call him back. She puts the message on the chancellor's desk with the rest of his mail.

Sunday Morning
The front page of the local section of the newspaper carries an article about a parent alleging that his son, a minor, has been molested by a priest. The reporter, unable to contact anyone at the chancery over the weekend, writes a carefully worded article.

The identities of the alleged victim and his family are protected. The name of the accused priest is not used. People read only that the accused is a Catholic priest and that the parents have been unable to get any response from the bishop or the chancellor of the diocese, both of whom are named in the article.

At this point in the hypothetical case, the situation would deteriorate rapidly. Control of the situation has passed from the chancery into the hands of the media and the lawyer—whom the priest would certainly retain. The sad thing is that no one in the chancery was acting maliciously, but everyone was dropping the ball. Unfortunately, this scenario is not a complete fabrication but is based upon actual situations in this country. It is the nightmare that diocesan communications directors dread.

A Five-Point Response

The following is a five-point plan for officially responding to accusations of sexual abuse within a diocese or religious congregation, and, by extrapolation, within the larger church:

1. Establish media crisis teams. Sexual scandals should not be handled by any one person in an institution; a team approach is advisable. Some dioceses establish media crisis teams which include such key persons as: the bishop, chancellor, vicar general, communications director, lawyer, and one or two other diocesan officials. This team approach ensures that someone will always be available to respond, unlike the above scenario where the responsibility fell on one absent person. Also, this team approach brings several good minds to bear on a stressful situation and, it is hoped, a more balanced and complete response.

2. Provide an immediate and personal response. The response needs to be immediate for both legal and pastoral reasons. In this author's home diocese of Orlando, Florida, state law requires that knowledge of child abuse be reported immediately to the State Human Resource Services. The Diocese of Orlando has its own additional guidelines as to how abuse must be reported.

In the above scenario, the chancellor failed to offer immediate and personal, pastoral care to a distraught father and his family in a crisis situation. He, or a representative of the diocese, should visit the family and assure them of the church's concern for their pain and offer its healing services. The accused priest also needs a personal visit. If he is guilty, he will need therapeutic help; if not, he still needs a support system and, perhaps, a lawyer.

In the case of a priest-pedophile, the damage to the morale of fellow priests can be severe. The bishop is the only one who can respond to this erosion in morale. The priests are looking for the bishop to be available to them, to be direct, and to assure them of his concern and support.

The bishop may or may not be personally available to other people affected by the crisis; his role is a judgment call. There are cases that are so public and so horrendous as to demand a personal response from the highest authority. In other cases, a personal response by members of the crisis team is sufficient. We do well to remember that the bishop is the avenue of last resort. His personal presence may be saved for a later moment.

Often, parents perceive that there is more institutional help for the perpetrator than for the victim. Church leaders must walk the tightrope of responding pastorally to both the victim and the accused.

3. Remove the accused. At the first indication of a problem, the diocese should remove the risk. If the accused pedophile is a priest, he must be temporarily suspended in such a way as to protect any potential future victims. This could mean a two-week vacation or sick leave. If the person is a teacher, he or she must leave the school. This may seem too harsh or tantamount to an admission of guilt. But if the charges are true, the pedophile must be taken out of a situation that will enable him to harm more children. It is a necessary protection for other potential victims.

Even if the accused is immediately removed, other parents will still be understandably angry and fearful that their children may also have been victims. Some parents may become hysterical and others will pursue the case out of a prurient interest. And there are still others who will use the situation as an excuse to vent their hostility toward the church and its priesthood. But, in general, well-meaning parents simply want the reassurance that a pedophile will not be in a position, ever again, to harm other children.

If the charges are not true, removal, even if temporary, protects the bishop from future allegations of negligence in not taking reasonable precautions when first alerted to a problem. It likewise assures the parents and community that the church is taking the situation seriously and making every effort to protect the children entrusted to its care.

4. Designate a spokesperson and draft a public statement. Once the news is in the public arena, it demands a public response. Total containment is impossible, but controlling the story's momentum is not. A direct and honest response can help to diffuse a rapidly escalating anger and suspicion directed at the church.

The media crisis team should meet, assess the situation, and decide on the content of the response and a spokesperson. The importance of this person cannot be overstated. As a communications director, I would advise colleagues and parishioners of the accused as well as diocesan officials to refer all media inquiries to the designated spokesperson. This person would probably not be the diocesan attorney, although all public statements should be checked with the attorney before being released.

A well-composed statement is essential. Sad experience warns us that a comment too profuse in its defense of the institution or of the accused often comes back to haunt the church. The statement should be pastoral in nature and state the truth as it is known. If the news is widespread, a press conference is in order. The statement should be on paper and read verbatim by the spokesperson who then offers to answer questions.

This initial exchange with the media may only be the beginning. Negative stories about the church are like cats: they have multiple lives and pounce on you when you least expect it. We had an example of a pedophilia case that had wide local media coverage because it was scheduled for trial. It was eventually settled out of court. Later, it was mentioned as part of a national newspaper article on pedophilia in the Catholic church, and almost a year later it appeared as part of an ABC television program, "20/20." This kind of "ripple" effect is not uncommon.

5. Tell the truth. It is extremely important to tell the truth. Secrecy, silence, or unavailability on the part of church leaders only adds to the anger and suspicion of the community. For too long the church has relied on its historical pattern of institutional secrecy. This is one case where it must "go public," at least to the extent of making sure the incident is reported to civil authorities. The church should never lie to newspeople, or attempt to cover up its own failings by diverting attention to the weak points of other people or institutions. It may be true that there is some "Catholic-bashing" in the news media, but we do ourselves a disservice when we are not direct and candid about our own failings. Efforts to prepare a cover up are not only morally unacceptable, they are also counterproductive.

Ending It All
A communications director and the entire media team must be sensitive to the ongoing damage done to the morale of the diocese and parish communities. Negative stories, especially about priests, carry the overwhelming temptation to develop "tunnel vi-

sion"—to see the entire church as sick, secretive, and reprehensible. On the other hand, there is nothing unhealthier than pretending that we are perfect or without weakness.

At such times, it is important to put equal emphasis on the "Good News" of our church and the good work that people accomplish. A communications director may need to concentrate on getting balancing stories out into the media. This helps to restore equilibrium to the public's perception and rebuilds internal morale.

There are those in the church who feel that we should be unconcerned about the image we project to the rest of the community. They say, "Our track record speaks for itself; we should apologize to no one." But of all institutions, the church should know the value and importance of genuine sorrow and repentance. When it comes to the issue of sexual scandals in the church, especially pedophilia, we must say that we are sorry and say it publicly. That sorrow is directed toward the victim, the pedophile, and our own institutional failures. Anything less spells a retreat to a time and an understanding of church built more on secrecy and defensiveness than on openness and compassion for all persons caught in such a tragic web.

Legal Aspects
of the Sexual Abuse of Children

Rev. Alan J. Placa, J.D.

A Legal *Apologia*

It is sad, but true, that in our society people who would offer "legal analyses" of social problems and policies must begin with an apology for our whole legal system. The need is justified, to some extent, by the apparent excesses of the legal system and the legal profession, and the need is made more dramatic by what has often been our own negative experience of "the Law." Consider these first paragraphs, then, as the mandatory *apologia* for what many see as an irrational patchwork, a crazy quilt of arbitrary rules and regulations formulated by people whose purposes are often seen as the obfuscation of simple issues and their own material enrichment.

Without denying that there are some unworthy practitioners of the legal profession (and of every other profession as well), let me assert vigorously that "the Law" is one of the most noble achievements of the human race. In particular, the U. S. legal system strives to incorporate the most fundamental values that we share as a people. I am well aware of the moral conflicts that find themselves enshrined in the law of our pluralistic society. But for those who have a vision of a more perfect society, a society without ethical disagreements and varying moral systems, let me try to elaborate that vision by way of offering a caution against it.

Imagine a society where all men and women share a single moral vision: where there is unanimity of mind and heart on questions of "good and evil," "right and wrong." Imagine a society where people speak one language, worship one God, and share common respect for each other's identities and destinies. You are as capable as I am of making such a society sound very desirable. Once we had described such a "unitary society," we would have described precisely the sort of society our ancestors came here to escape. Our Catholic ancestors came here to escape the "unitary societies" of European Protestantism. Our Protestant ancestors came here to escape the "unitary societies" of European Catholicism, and our Jewish ancestors came here simply to escape what was being done to them all over Europe.

Our ancestors came here to declare, solemnly, that never again would they allow the government to inquire into questions of personal moral values: we insist that these are questions that we will work out in the voluntary communities that we form within the larger society. Whether the principle of "occult compensation" is morally viable, whether transubstantiation is true, or whether canon law is a fair system to regulate interpersonal relations are not questions open to governmental scrutiny. We decide and deal with these issues *privately*, and our ancestors were willing to risk all and to pay dearly for that right.

But none of this implies that we have created a society of mutually exclusive cultures which never interact with one another. It has been the genius of U. S. society (and the source of U. S. prosperity) that there is a willingness to enter into commerce and conversation with all sorts of people. We have carefully, even painfully, developed a common language which addresses issues of shared concern while it cautiously and respectfully avoids issues of "private" or "sectarian" concern. This new "common language" is the law. U. S. law is the system we have devised for communicating with each other and holding ourselves and each other accountable to certain public standards.

While the law cannot interfere with my *beliefs*, it can and must concern itself with my *behavior*. When people claim that their beliefs require them to act in a way that we as a society find unacceptable, the law must intervene, holding each and every individual and group in society to the rules of discourse we have hammered out in the political process. When Mormons claimed that men should be permitted to have many wives, for example, the law intervened. (Now they cannot.) When some Native Americans claimed that certain narcotic drugs were "sacraments" of their religion, the law intervened. (They can use otherwise "illegal" substances under special conditions.) When behavior which I claim springs from my beliefs is challenged, I cannot defend my behavior by appealing to the "private language" of religion or ethnicity: I must explain the rightness of my acts by entering into a dialogue framed in the common language of the law.

We are concerned, then, about the legal aspects of the issue of child sexual abuse precisely because we want to understand the state of public social policy on the issue. We want to be responsible members of our complex society, taking an active role in shaping social policy and being willing to be held accountable to the policy we shape.

In the area of social policies concerning sexual behavior, the church has an important role to play. It is essential that we be active participants in the political dialogue that shapes public policy in our state legislatures, especially because we have the valuable contribution of our 2000-year tradition of moral reflection to offer. It is interesting to observe that in an age of "sexual liberty," more public attention is focused on controlling sexual behavior than ever before. In addition to the widely publicized concern over the sexual abuse of children, there are many legal actions (both criminal and civil) initiated for "sexual harassment," "spousal rape," "date rape," "alienation of affection" (in the jurisdictions where that cause of action still exists), and for "intentional infliction of emotional distress" in cases where individuals claim they were intentionally harmed by the sexual acts of others. Nor is the interest in controlling sexual behavior limited to the courtroom: state legislatures, prompted by various advocacy groups, are constantly reviewing criminal laws governing sexual activity.

The key to understanding this increased legal interest in sexual behavior is the concept of *consent*, particularly, the conditions that may mitigate a person's capacity to consent freely to sexual acts. In some cases, courts must hear subtle and complex testimony to determine the capacity of consent of the alleged victim and/or the nature and extent of the power and pressure exerted by the accused person. In the case of child sexual abuse, however, the matter is considerably more simple. Every state offers a very simple

definition: no person below a specified age is ever free to consent
to a sexual act of any kind. The vast majority of states identify this
"age of capacity" as beginning with a person's eighteenth birthday.

Such an arbitrary definition, expressed in every state's legal
system, reveals the extent to which our society is committed to a
social policy which seeks to protect "children." Many people find
a lack of sensitivity to the rights of young people in such definitions. Certainly, many people find that significant mechanisms for
the protection of accused persons have been eroded in cases
where the accusation involves the sexual abuse of children. While
there may or may not be merit to these observations, they serve to
emphasize the lengths to which our society is willing to go in its
efforts to protect the young.

The Church's Concerns

This same concern for the young is at the heart of the church's interest in the matter of the sexual abuse of children. It is sometimes
cynically observed that the church has much at stake in these issues because of the large financial awards made by juries in the
handful of much publicized cases involving ministers of religion
who have been found guilty of molesting children. The church's
real concern, however, is much deeper.

Every day, hundreds of thousands of children are in the care of
"the church" in the United States. From 24-hours-a-day settings
like orphanages and foster homes, through our system of Catholic
schools, religious education, social and cultural programs, athletic
activities, and even the half-hour contact of an altar server at
morning Mass, *children are entrusted to the church.* Children have
learned to trust, respect, and even to love our priests, religious sisters and brothers, lay employees, and volunteers, and for good
reason: the vast majority of these men and women are capable,
compassionate, trustworthy adults whose only concern is for the
well-being of the children entrusted to their care. Our personnel
are well-situated—perhaps uniquely well-situated—to be the first
people to whom children will turn for help when they are suffering. And let us make no mistake about it: in spite of our material
comfort, children are suffering in our country. A brief conversation with an attending physician in the emergency room of any
large metropolitan hospital will reveal the extent to which chil-

dren are being physically and emotionally abused in their own homes, by their own parents, guardians, and relatives in our society.

It is very important to understand that the story of child sexual abuse in the U. S. and Canada is essentially the same: children are being sexually abused in their own homes, by close relatives, and by persons who have the complete trust of parents and guardians. The lurid headlines describing isolated incidents of a priest, or religious brother, or Boy Scout leader molesting a young boy give a dangerously inaccurate impression: they make it seem that "the problem" is that trusted public figures are taking sexual advantage of boys. "The problem" of child sexual abuse is something quite different: girls and young women are being sexually molested by members of their own households.

Certainly the church has a responsibility to be concerned for the scandal generated when people in ministry misconduct themselves sexually. Certainly the church has a responsibility to protect the assets entrusted to its stewardship so that the Gospel may be preached and so that Christian charity may be exercised. But the truth of the matter (a truth I have learned and come to believe through the nearly two hundred cases in which I have been involved in the last ten years) is that _the church really is concerned for the children entrusted to its care._ The church wants all of its personnel to understand the clinical and the social policy dimensions of the problem of child abuse so that they will be able to intervene to protect children, to heal them, and to minister effectively to their families and to those who are accused of molesting them.

The church is concerned for all of the aspects of child abuse which society addresses in its laws: the physical abuse, emotional abuse, sexual abuse, and neglect of children. And the church is concerned for aspects of the harm caused by abuse that the state cannot hope to address: the spiritual harm done to children. The church is concerned with the lack of trust and hope that result from the betrayal which is child abuse.

One of the most important ways the church expresses these concerns is by providing for special training for church personnel. We all need to be trained to recognize the medical and behavioral manifestations of abuse. We need, too, to understand the implications of social policy: the "child-abuse reporting laws" (which have been passed throughout the U. S. in the past 15 years), the implications of these statutes for "clergy confidentiality" and the "seal of confession," and the legal processes to which victims, their families, and accused persons are exposed once a report of child abuse is made. Effective ministry means recognizing the manifestations of abuse in a child too frightened to speak; it means knowing how to respond to a child who does choose to speak; and it means having a pastorally sensitive appreciation of the pressures the legal system will place on all persons involved in the process.

The Legal Processes

There are potentially three distinct kinds of legal processes involved in cases of child sexual abuse: a series of *investigative* processes, a *criminal* process, and a *civil* process.[1]

The initial investigative process is undertaken by a state or provincial social welfare agency in response to a report of child abuse. Each of the fifty states has enacted some statute requiring the reporting of incidents of physical, emotional, or sexual abuse of children. In every case, these statutes have a single purpose: to overcome all barriers to uncovering abusive behavior. Some of the conditions which might preclude a person from reporting abuse include lack of knowledge of complex, bureaucratic reporting procedures; a fear that the report might turn out to be untrue and that the reporter would then be indicted for defamation of character; or a concern that such a report might constitute a breach of professional confidentiality.

Most states have tried to address these three problems in their reporting mechanisms. The usual scheme involves the creation of a new state agency, or the extension of the mandate of an existing state agency (for the sake of convenience we will refer to these as "Child Protective Service" agencies) to include the investigation of reports. Many states have established "800" telephone numbers for a "reporting hotline." This means that ordinary citizens have immediate, free access to the agency charged with investigating reports of child abuse. The reporting system is as simple as picking up a telephone and making a toll-free call.

To my knowledge, throughout the U. S. persons who make reports of child abuse are protected against all legal processes based on their reports, except in the case of malicious reports. In other words, if a person makes a "hotline" report of suspected child abuse (physical, emotional, or sexual), and that suspicion turns out to be unfounded, the person who made the report cannot be subjected to criminal charges or to a civil lawsuit for money damages unless it can be shown that the report was made maliciously for the purpose of harassing the accused person.

Finally, all states have suspended the ordinary laws governing "privileged" or "confidential" relationships in favor of the reporting of suspected incidents of child abuse. Most protect the communications made in the course of certain professional relationships. People are assured by law that when they tell all of the truth to their physicians, their lawyers, or their ministers of religion, this information is absolutely confidential and may never be revealed by the professional person in whom they confided. All have modified the extent of that protection by asserting that suspected incidents of child abuse *must* be reported, and that such reports do not constitute a breach of the confidentiality protected by law.

Reporting Laws

Although each State has its own particular statutory scheme for reporting child abuse, there are two broad categories of reporting laws. Some have reporting laws which require that *certain specified persons* make these reports when they have "reason to believe"[2] that a child has been abused. New York's reporting statute is an example of this kind of law. Section 413 of New York State's Social Services Law requires the following persons to report abuse: physicians, surgeons, medical examiners, coroners, dentists, osteopaths, optometrists, chiropractors, podiatrists, (medical) residents, (medical) interns, psychologists, registered nurses, hospital personnel engaged in the admission, examination, care, or treatment of persons, Christian Science practitioners, school officials, social services workers, daycare center workers or any other childcare or fostercare workers, mental health professionals, peace officers, police officers, and law-enforcement officials.[3] Failure to make a required report is a misdemeanor in New York, and may be punished by six months imprisonment, or a fine of $1000, or both. In addition, state agencies that license or certify professionals may investigate the failure to report, and the professional may be subject to suspension or loss of a license or certificate.

Other states have more broadly worded statutes that require that *"any person"* must make a report when he or she has "reason to believe" that a child has been abused. Since these statutes have wider application, failure to obey them generally carries fewer penalties than the statutes that incorporate a specific list of mandated reporters.

In any event, once a hotline report is made under either of these two kinds of statutes, the state's Child Protective Services or "CPS" agency must undertake an investigation. If such a report were made against me, as a priest, for example, employees of my state's CPS would present themselves at my rectory asking for a list of the names and addresses of the parish's altar boys (or other children with whom I might have had contact). Armed with that list, the CPS investigators would visit each family indicated and ask to interview the children to determine whether they had been molested by their parish priest.[4]

Before we go further in discussing the legal processes involved, please note that this investigative process is, of itself, very damaging to the person accused. Whether the accusation is true or false, once the possibility of child abuse by a priest (or a teacher, or a physician, or a scout leader) has been raised in people's minds, this concern will spread like wildfire, making it impossible for the accused person to continue to work effectively in that community.

If the CPS investigation determines that the report is "unfounded," then most state statutory schemes require that all records of the report and investigation be expunged from the state's "central register" of child abuse reports and investigations. On the other hand, if the investigation concludes that the report is "founded," CPS is required to turn the matter over to the local prosecutor or district attorney. District attorneys are elected officials, and their function is to evaluate the quality of evidence gathered and to exercise "prosecutorial discretion" in making a decision to prosecute or not to prosecute an accused person. In most cases, a district attorney will use police officers to conduct further investigation (many localities have specifically trained "sex crimes units" to conduct such investigations).

It would be a mistake to believe that district attorneys exercise their "prosecutorial discretion" solely on the basis of professional judgments: there is a large measure of political expediency involved in the process. The best and most honest prosecutors know that accusations of child sexual abuse are potentially explosive. District attorneys who undertake such prosecutions may find themselves at the center of time-consuming and highly publicized controversies in their communities. Those who choose not to prosecute may find that the public will question their zeal and competence in the next election.[5]

The Criminal Process

If the district attorney decides that the quality of the evidence is sufficient to bring the matter to trial, the case enters into the criminal process. In such an event, the accused person stands in danger of losing his or her liberty: child sexual abuse is a felony, and acts of abuse can lead to lengthy imprisonment. In order to obtain a conviction, the prosecutor must prove that the accused person is guilty *"beyond a reasonable doubt."* Achieving this very high level of proof is always a difficult matter, and North America's legal systems go to great lengths to protect the rights of accused persons. In the area of accusations of child sexual abuse, however, many of the traditional protections of the rights of the accused have been modified or mitigated.

For example, child abuse is an accusation that need not be corroborated in order to be brought to trial. Ordinarily, courts will not allow the vast expenditures of public money required to stage a trial simply to hear an accuser assert "He did it," and an accused person respond "No, I didn't," without further evidence or corroboration. In the case of child sexual abuse, however, it is felt that secrecy and lack of corroboration are part of the nature of the crime, and it is deemed unfair to fail to prosecute for lack of corroboration.

Another traditional defense against criminal charges is an *alibi*, e.g., "I was elsewhere" at the time the crime was allegedly committed. This traditional defense is of only limited use to defendants in child abuse cases. Many states have amended their evidence codes; an alleged child-victim need not be able to remember the exact time and place of the acts since requiring such precision of recollection is considered an unfair burden on a child.

Civil Lawsuits

In spite of all these limitations, however, proof "beyond a reasonable doubt" is still a difficult standard, and many criminal prosecutions fall short of the mark, ending in acquittal. It would be a mistake, however, to believe that an acquittal means the end of the ordeal for the child who has been interrogated time and time again, for the child's family, for the accused person, or for the community. In addition to the criminal prosecution involved, there may also be a *civil lawsuit* for money damages pending.

The *criminal* action usually bears a title such as "The People of the State versus John Smith," and John Smith is accused of offending the common welfare of all the people; for such an offense John Smith may be deprived of his liberty. A *civil* suit addressing the same subject bears a title such as "William and Mary Jones, on Behalf of their Infant Son, James, versus John Smith." In such a civil action, John Smith is accused of doing measurable harm to certain individuals in society. While he is not in danger of losing his liberty, he is liable for money damages to pay for the harm he is accused of inflicting on those individuals.

Some may wonder whether the bringing of two legal actions (one criminal and one civil) constitutes "double jeopardy" and is thus forbidden by the U. S. Constitution. It does not. Constitutional principles protect us from being put "twice in jeopardy of life or liberty." A civil suit seeks only money damages, not capital punishment or imprisonment, and thus does not violate the prohibition against "double jeopardy."

It may also occur to some people that a civil suit subsequent to a criminal trial which ended in acquittal is pointless: the accused person has already been found "not guilty," so why try him or her again?

There may be good reason to try a subsequent civil action because the standards of proof are different in criminal and civil actions. In order to have the accused person imprisoned for a criminal offense, the prosecutor must prove guilt "beyond a reasonable doubt." In a civil suit, however, the plaintiff only needs to establish the defendant's liability by the lower standard of *"the preponderance of the evidence."* In many cases, the evidence collected is insufficient to meet the higher criminal standard, but is enough to get a judgment for money damages.[6]

We have all heard and read of the enormous money judgments that have been rendered against churches and other organizations because their employees have been involved in child abuse. How is it that an organization can be held responsible for the acts of its employees or other representatives? We understand that a trucking company may be held liable for damage done by one of its drivers who was performing the duties of his employment while driving a company truck, but certainly no one can claim that sexual molestation is encompassed in the "scope of duty" of any person. Although there are subtle legal arguments to sustain liability on the part of the employer, perhaps an anecdote will make the point more clearly.

I once worked on a case in a small midwestern diocese. A priest had been accused of molesting an adolescent boy in his parish, and the local bishop had invited me to come and attempt to resolve the matter without recourse to legal process. I interviewed the priest, the boy, and the boy's parents separately. The meeting with the parents was rather tense, but they were good and sincere people, and they wanted to help their son and protect other youngsters without exposing their child and their whole family to the legal process. There was a momentary lull in the conversation, and the boy's father stood up, approached me, and lifted me out of my chair by the lapels of my black coat. He said, "You son of a bitch, how could you have let this happen? You're my family. I trusted you." I was a complete stranger in that place, and the man wasn't addressing me personally; he was expressing his feeling that he and his family had been betrayed by an institution which he had trusted, an institution which my clerical garb represented to him at that moment.

No lawyer could give better expression to the legal grounds for finding institutional liability in these matters. Those parents reasonably relied on "the church." They entrusted their son to the priest in question not because they knew or trusted him personally (although they may have known him well), but because the priest was clothed in the moral authority of the institution he represented. Courts will often find that this "reasonable reliance" on the part of innocent people is sufficient to find that an institution had a duty to protect innocent third parties from the misconduct of its agents.

Statutes of Limitations

One last procedural issue is worth noting. Most people know that there are such things as "statutes of limitations" which prevent legal actions from being brought after the passage of a certain period of time. In connection with the issue of child abuse, the question of the applicable statute of limitations arises in two ways. In the first place, people who are dealing with those who claim they were victims of child abuse ask whether they are required to report such incidents when they believe that the term of the statute of limitations may have already passed. Second, people who are dealing with adults who may have committed acts of abuse would like to know when the statute of limitations will give some sense of "repose," some "peace of mind" to such people.

To both of these questions, let me begin by commenting that statutes of limitation are more subtle, more complex, and more difficult to calculate than they might at first appear. Because of these complexities, my advice to a mandated reporter would be to avoid considering the question of statutes of limitations altogether, and make the mandated report. It should be kept in mind that the initiation of legal proceedings against abusers is only one purpose of the reporting laws. These laws also mandate systems for treating victims and for protecting possible future victims.

When the focus is on the situation of the alleged abuser, a more complicated analysis is necessary if we are to understand statutes of limitations. A statute of limitations has two purposes. First, it is meant to make lawsuits more efficient and fair by avoiding bringing "stale" issues into court. It would be very difficult to prove the truth or falsehood of an issue which allegedly took place twenty years ago: people's memories dim, witnesses die, documents are lost, etc. Second, statutes of limitations are meant to give some measure of "repose" to potential defendants (in both criminal and civil actions).

It should be kept in mind that statutes of limitations for criminal offenses are generally longer than those for civil lawsuits. In other words, the state has a longer "window of opportunity" for bringing criminals to justice than private citizens have for being compensated for personal damages. In the U. S., a typical statutory scheme in matters of child abuse would operate this way: the state has five years to bring a criminal action against the alleged offender, while private citizens have two years to commence civil suits against potential defendants.

Let's look at this time frame a bit more closely. If the alleged victim is a minor, then the "clock" of the statutes of limitations (criminal and civil) does not begin to "tick" until the alleged victim has reached legal majority (usually the eighteenth birthday). On the basis of that one refinement of the definition of the statute of limitations, then, it would seem that the state can bring a criminal action against an alleged offender until the alleged victim has reached his or her twenty-third birthday (i.e., five years after the achievement of legal majority).

Similarly, it would seem that the alleged victims can file civil lawsuits for money damages against alleged offenders (and against associated institutional defendants, where appropriate) until they reach their twentieth birthdays (i.e., two years after the achievement of legal majority). But, again, it is not quite so simple. For example, the "clock stops ticking" when the potential defendant is physically outside of the state's jurisdiction (for something more than a short vacation). This is why lawsuits often begin with protracted hearings about the applicability of the statute of limitations: it is often necessary to enter a great deal of evidence on this question before the legal action can actually commence.

There is a further complication. Although statutes of limitations in criminal actions are interpreted rather strictly (after all, a person's liberty is at stake), statutes of limitations in civil matters are sometimes analyzed with a bit more liberality. Based on reasoning developed in several western states, some people now say that there will soon be no effective statute of limitations for bringing civil lawsuits for money damages against individual and institutional defendants. In fact, this prediction is based on a series of California cases[7] that have held that the statute of limitations in cases of child sexual abuse ought to be interpreted the same way as in cases of medical malpractice. In those cases, the statutes' "clock" does not start "ticking" until "a reasonable person should have known of the harm." The reason for this analysis is that acts of medical malpractice often involve harm that an ordinary person could not possibly be aware of for many years after the act occurs.

If a small sponge or small surgical instrument, for example, is sewn up inside of a surgical field during abdominal surgery, the patient might not be aware of the problem for years, until the foreign object punctured an organ, or until an x-ray taken for some other reason revealed the presence of the foreign object. At that moment, a "reasonable person" should be aware that something went wrong, and the statutes of limitations' "clock" starts to "tick" at that moment, regardless of how long ago the surgeon's error took place.

The California courts see an analogy to the medical malpractice rule for interpreting the statutes of limitations when plantiffs can argue successfully either that they did not understand that the act committed was wrong, or that demonstrable psychological mechanisms have prevented them from facing the meaning of past acts. The California appellate court in the *Evans* case (referred to in note 7) holds that since "parents . . . [s]tepparents, foster parents, and others in positions of parental authority" have "confidential" relationships with children, relations which "plac[e] special duties on the[m] . . . for the protection of the child's health and well-being, as well as special rights of custody and control," these adults have special power over children. Children may have no choice but to acquiesce in their acts. Furthermore, that kind of acquiescence may be buried deep in a victim's mind, making the person unable for many years to evaluate the acts performed.

If we consider that church personnel are often people who are "in positions of parental authority," it should be plain that as this "California rule" becomes accepted in other parts of our country (as many lawyers, myself among them, believe it will), allegations of misconduct from years and even decades ago may be legally made against such persons.

A Pastoral Response

Everyone in our society is affected by the problem of child abuse. Because the church is genuinely concerned about the welfare of children, church leaders in our country are anxious to develop an appropriate pastoral response to the sufferings of abused children. One important element in developing such a pastoral response is the sponsorship of educational programs in this area. Dioceses and religious congregations ought to invite medical and mental health clinicians to address their personnel in order to familiarize them with the clinical manifestations of child abuse, so that personnel can intervene to help children who are hurt. They ought also to invite attorneys to describe the social policy dimensions of the question of child abuse, so that ministerial personnel can be prepared to act in the best interests of victims and be aware of their own responsibilities under the law.

When we consider the possibility that some of our own colleagues and co-ministers may be involved in the abuse of children (however few actually are involved, and however low the statistical probabilities), there are things that should be done. In the first place, we ought to be encouraging one another to behave more and more prudently. Many fine things that we did twenty years ago should not be done today, precisely because the environment has changed. We might go so far as to say that the atmosphere has been poisoned by the fact that we now know that children are being abused.

Consider the church minister who is perceived as "king of the kids," who has no significant peer relationships, but spends all of his time with youngsters, who takes kids on trips and vacations, who invites kids into his private room in a residence. Years ago, such a person might have been seen as a valuable minister, a person selflessly dedicated to the young. Today, those behavior patterns are profoundly imprudent and, quite simply, unacceptable. Let me emphasize that I am not a clinician, and I am not implying that such behavior patterns are "symptoms" of anything. As a lawyer and as a priest, I am saying that anyone who lives this way should be challenged by his co-ministers and/or his superiors.

Twenty years ago, when a young person shared the story of some personal suffering with me, I reached out to embrace him, confident that the embrace would be understood as an appropriate expression of concern and support. Today, I am not sure who the last adult male was who embraced that young person and I am not sure what that person did. I cannot risk having my innocent acts misconstrued; I cannot risk frightening or alienating a young person in need of help. This seems to mean that we are walking a fine line between searching for appropriate expressions of our spontaneous emotions, and appearing to be cold and impersonal. But that is the challenge we face today: we must be much more sensitive to the people who confide in us; we must try to know them more deeply before we decide what will be an appropriate and acceptable expression of our feelings; we must implicitly seek their "permission" to do things that might be misconstrued.

Finally, we must be prepared with a truly pastoral response if and when an accusation is made against one of our co-ministers (clergy, religious, or lay). Church ministry is an honorable profession, and it has its own skills. We should trust our ministerial skills and instincts in responding to such allegations. For instance, if a parent came to the door of any rectory, convent, or friary and reported that a child had been molested, I am sure I know what the response should be: our colleagues would welcome the parent, express compassion, and offer help (for instance, a referral would be made to a Catholic Charities agency for psychological counseling of some sort for the child and for the whole family). I am relatively certain that the priest, sister, or brother who answered the door would not grill the parent, asking for proof of the allegation. I hope and pray that I am right in assuming that the person answering the door would not "clam up" and say that it would be "improper" to get involved. And yet, those are precisely the negative and even adversarial postures that are often taken when such an allegation is made against "one of our own."

Analyze the issue this way: when a child says that he or she has been sexually abused, one of two things holds—the allegation is either *true* or *false*. If the allegation is *true*, then the child is suffering because he or she has been abused. If the accusation is *false*, then the child is suffering in some other way, because (aside from patently malicious undertakings) children do not say such things without reason. In fact, even the child who is lying in a patently malicious way is in need of some kind of help. And that is the point: whether the allegation is true or false, *the child making the allegation needs some kind of help.* If an agent of the Roman Catholic church offers help openly and sincerely to a person who needs it, I can assure you that no untoward legal consequences will follow upon that ministerial intervention.

In former times, the church's response was often cold, hostile, and adversarial. Church officials often insisted that a supervised meeting be held between the child-accuser and the accused adult. Such meetings often led to a reprimand of the priest or religious involved, followed by the "geographical solution"—a transfer to a different assignment. The first time I heard a church official say he was going to arrange such a meeting, I gasped and asked why. The answer came quickly, "Because we have a right to be confronted by our accusers, Father." Well, we certainly do have such a right—*in court*. Why, in heaven's name, would we be talking "court language?" Like the midwestern father, I described earlier, these people come to us looking for their "family." If they find juridical entities who propose holding kangaroo courts, how will they respond?[8] Certainly they know where to find real courts where their interests will be protected, and they will deal with church officials on (at least) an equal footing.

A Christ-like Response

So, then, how should we respond? Is it too simple to say that church ministers should respond like church ministers? Is it too obvious to say that we should respond in a Christ-like way, offering help to people who are suffering for whatever reason? Please understand, I do not mean that a quick referral to Catholic Charities should be the end of the matter. Religious superiors must be informed. Dioceses and religious congregations must have policies and procedures in place to offer appropriate assistance and to protect the interests of the church. But the starting point must be for us to respond with the compassion people have a right to expect from the church. Our response, individually and institutionally, must clearly express our priorities. I suggest that when allegations of this kind are made against our own personnel, these must be our priorities:

1. A clear concern for the alleged victim, expressed through compassionate offers of assistance.

2. A realistically expressed concern for potential future victims (and this concern may well imply temporary removal of the accused person from his or her assignment until the matter can be properly investigated and sorted out).

3. A concern for the interests of the church; as a lawyer I am not ashamed to admit that I have a concern for protecting the assets of the church, the assets with which the church is supposed to minister to the needs of so many. As a priest I am painfully aware that the church's interests go far beyond its material interests. If one of us has misconducted himself in this way, I want to see to it that the other 50,000 or so priests and religious men in the U. S., for example, are not deprived, by scandal, of the opportunity to continue the good and wholesome work they are doing.

4. A fraternal and Christian concern for the accused person, including a concern that the accused person receive any clinical and/or legal help that may be needed.

Reintegration into Ministry

Can a person who has been involved in sexual activity with youngsters ever be reintegrated into church ministry again? Can such a person ever be trusted to represent the church again? Predictably, ages simpler than our own had simple answers for these questions.

In the age of the "geographical solution," there was a simple answer: Yes. Such a person could be returned to active ministry after disciplinary and moral measures had been taken, and after the person had been moved far away from the place where the scandalous acts occurred. This was really very simple. Sexual misconduct of all kinds was lumped together as a moral and disciplinary problem. A person found to be involved in this sort of activity was withdrawn from ministry and sent off for some sort of penance (Trappist monasteries were popular sites for this), and then was returned to active ministry in an area distant from his last assignment with a stern warning from the bishop or provincial.

Of course, since this methodology did not address the underlying clinical issues, it did little or no good. To be fair, we must observe that it was not only religious superiors who failed to address the underlying clinical issues; thirty years ago even clinicians did not properly understand the mechanisms behind sexual interest in young children. In any event, the "geographical solution" was not likely to work: the man "punished" and "exiled" would probably act out again. In today's litigious atmosphere, such recidivism would be disastrous. A suit against a diocese or province for negligence asserts, "You should have known, but didn't, you fool," but a suit triggered by recidivism is a suit for recklessness, and would assert, "You did know, but did nothing appropriate about it, you *scoundrel*." In court, "negligent fools" are liable for payments whose purpose is to compensate the injured party for loss. "Reckless scoundrels," on the other hand, must compensate their victims and must also be punished for their recklessness. In many states they are required to pay "treble" damages—a certain amount to compensate for losses plus twice that amount as a punishment for recklessness.

Once the inefficacy of the "geographical solution" was widely recognized, bishops and major superiors were inclined simply to say that no one who had ever been involved in sexual activity with youngsters could ever be reintegrated into church ministry. Several painful attempts to dismiss priests from the clerical state, and several procedures to dismiss professed members of religious congregations are sad but eloquent testimony to this period of frightened overreaction to an earlier time when church leaders had unbounded confidence in the power of their penal measures to change the offender.

Today's church leaders, like today's clinicians, are better informed about the meaning of sexual misconduct, and they are more aware of the need to understand the clinical picture before deciding about ministry reintegration.

For example, if, after residential therapy has been completed, a person is diagnosed as a fixated pedophile, the bishop or major superior should not attempt to reintegrate such a person into ministry. This diagnosis indicates a serious mental illness, whereby a person has no sexual interest at all other than the prepubescent children.[9]

For other sexual offenders, however, the matter is not so simple. In the first place, we are very much dependent on clinical judgments in our attempt to make assignment decisions. What is to be done with the man who, on one or two isolated occasions, has misconducted himself sexually with young children, but who is not diagnosed as a fixated pedophile? What is to be done with the man who has misconducted himself sexually with young people, but is an ephebophile rather than a pedophile?

Suggestions for Ministry Reintegration

Looking at these questions of reintegration into ministry, as a priest and an attorney, I offer the following observations and guidelines:

1. Residential Care Anyone who has been involved in sexual misconduct should be involved in a course of residential, therapeutic care. Living the celibate life is so much at the heart of our vocations as priests and religious that a person who has engaged in inappropriate and harmful sexual activity must have professional assistance in re-evaluating his ability to continue in the celibate lifestyle.

2. Evaluation of Clinical Diagnosis and Prognosis The condition of a person who has misconducted himself sexually with youngsters will be described in one of three ways: fixated pedophilia, regressed pedophilia, or ephebophilia (sexual activity with adolescents). Religious superiors should look carefully at the clinician's description or diagnosis, and at the clinician's prognosis. The person diagnosed as a fixated pedophile should not, in my opinion, be readmitted to active ministry. Our dealing with him must be guided by fraternal charity, by the obligations imposed by general and particular church law, and by the customs and usages of religious congregations (where applicable). However, it would seem to me that any attempt to reintegrate a diagnosed fixated pedophile into ministry is reckless.

3. Reintegration into Ministry Persons who have misconducted themselves sexually with young people, but who have not been diagnosed as fixated pedophiles, may be reintegrated into ministry after a term of residential care, provided that the clinician's prognosis gives hope that the person will be able to func-

tion safely again. Assuming such a positive prognosis, I suggest
that a person may be reintegrated into ministry if, and only if, certain conditions are met:

Conditions for Reintegration

1. No Unsupervised Contact   There should be no unsupervised
contact with youngsters in the particular age group for a specified
period of time. This principle implies several things. First, it obviously means that a person cannot be assigned to an activity, such
as teaching or youth counseling, where it is the very nature of the
work to serve youngsters with a minimum of supervision. Second, it suggests that reassignment to a more generalized ministry
(such as parish work) will mean informing the immediate superi-
or (the pastor, for example) of the man's history. Also, the superi-
or should be made aware that this man is not to involve himself in
the sort of contact with young people that arises in the course of
ordinary ministry without the presence, help, and guidance of another staff member. In fact, this principle goes beyond contacts
with youngsters in the work place: it means that there should be
no unsupervised contact with youngsters of the problematic age
group, even in the individual's personal life.

2. Ongoing Individual Therapy   The person to be reintegrated into ministry must also commit himself to a course of ongoing,
individual therapy. The nature and frequency of the therapy will
be determined by the report and prognosis prepared by the clinicians who supervised the man's residential therapy. In any event,
the man must commit himself to continuing with the therapy suggested and must agree to execute formal "Waivers of Confidentiality" which will allow the treating clinician to make full reports
of the therapy to the bishop or other religious superior.

3. Twelve-Step Self-Help Groups   Based on the model of Alcoholics Anonymous, these groups (called "Sex and Love Addicts
Anonymous," "Sexaholics Anonymous," or a variety of other
names) help people with sexual compulsions (sometimes described as "sexual addictions") to modify their behavior. As with
A.A., these groups have achieved remarkable success. Local
groups of this kind are located in most larger cities in the U. S.
and Canada.

4. Appointment of a "Mentor" or "Supervisor"   In many ways,
this is the most important element of the reintegration into ministry. The "mentor" is not a person's therapist or spiritual director.

The mentor is a person who will have had some minimal orientation to the fundamental clinical understanding of sexual compulsions, but will remain simply a mentoring and supervising colleague.

The priest who is to be reintegrated into ministry must understand that he has caused pain to himself, to one or more young people, to church administrators, and to his colleagues in ministry. Reintegration implies that he will open his life up to fraternal scrutiny and will ask for help in finding his way back to fruitful and faithful ministry. He must understand that the mentor/ supervisor will meet with him regularly (frequency to be determined after consulting clinicians, including the therapist involved in the person's ongoing treatment) and will ask him to describe his contacts with, and his dreams and fantasies about, people of the targeted age group. The mentor's role is to supervise the person's contacts with youngsters in his own most personal life, and to intervene to break the cycles of compulsion that may again lead to trouble. The person must understand that the mentor/ supervisor is free to report his observations to religious superiors (but not to civil authorities), and that this openness is a condition for the attempt to reintegrate into ministry.

In my own experience, attempts to reintegrate people into ministry have been quite successful. I have never been involved in attempting to reintegrate a clinically diagnosed fixated pedophile into ministry, however. Similarly, I have never been involved in attempting to reintegrate a person into ministry after that person has been convicted of a criminal offense and has served time in prison. Such a move would be inappropriate, at the very least, for "public-relations" reasons, if not also for clinical, legal, and moral reasons. With these provisos in mind, I report that my own experience (in many cases over the last six years) leads me to believe that most people who have engaged in the sort of inappropriate behavior we are describing here can successfully be reintegrated into some useful and fulfilling church ministry.

Conclusion

The urgent problem of the sexual abuse of children in our society is tragic. In spite of the publicity given to the subject, many more children are being harmed than we realize. Also, in spite of the publicity, very few priests and religious are engaged in this kind of behavior. Although reliable statistics are difficult to find, a perusal of the reported legal actions in the U. S. shows that fewer than one-quarter of 1 percent of the priests and religious men have been involved in such actions. Certainly there are cases which never go to court, but even if that number is off by a factor of ten (and, based on my experience, I do not believe that is true) this is still a lower percentage than that of the adult male population involved in such abuse—even using the most conservative estimates.

The church needs to be an advocate for and protector of children, not only the children entrusted to its care, but of all children. The church can do this best by being true to its vocation, preaching vigorously its own authentic moral message of respect for others and for oneself, and encouraging all people to grow up to their full stature in Christ.

> If we live by the truth and in love, we shall grow in all ways into Christ, who is the head, by whom the whole body is fitted and joined together, every joint adding its own strength, for each separate part to work according to its function. So the body grows until it has built itself up, in love. *Ephesians 4:15–16.*

Notes

1. The purpose of this material is to give an overview and appreciation of the response of the U.S. legal system to the problem of child sexual abuse. It is important to understand that the laws of the fifty states and the District of Columbia differ significantly in this as in other areas. Interested individuals should seek specific legal advice only from attorneys admitted to practice in their own states.

2. Persons who are mandated to report express great concern over the phrase "reason to believe that a child has been abused." When does one have sufficient "reason to believe" to trigger the law's requirement that a report be made? As I hope will become clear, having "reason to believe" does not mean being absolutely certain of the truth of the accusation—determining the ultimate

truth or falsehood of the accusation is the job of the courts. Neither does it require that one undertake a complex investigation to evaluate the quality of the evidence of abuse—that is the job of the police and of the district attorney. Nor does it mean that one has made inquiries to determine whether there is any foundation at all to the accusation—that is the job of the state's child-welfare agencies. "Reason to believe," then, means that it is "not unreasonable" to believe that the child has been abused. That is a rather subjective standard, and it does vary from person to person. A licensed child psychologist, for example, may have the skill and experience to delve beyond a child's initial report to find that it is a mere fantasy (and so, that professional will not have "reason to believe" the child's story). Another person with fewer skills in communicating with children, on the other hand, may be unable to evaluate the child's story, and may have "reason to believe" the accusation immediately upon hearing it.

3. It is interesting and important to note that members of the "clergy" are not included in this particular list in New York's statute. A proper understanding of relevant reporting laws requires that you consult an attorney admitted to practice in your state or province. Some states do include the clergy in these lists, and they have a variety of definitions of "clergy." For example, are religious sisters, religious brothers, permanent deacons, or other church workers included in the definition?

4. The quality of these investigations tends to be somewhat spotty, at best. The persons conducting the investigations are not professional social workers, much less are they police officers or persons trained to understand and protect the rights of accused persons. In one state, the manual used to train these investigators instructs them to ask questions such as, "Did he touch you in a place where you would wear a bathing suit?" in order to learn whether or not an inappropriate contact was made.

The McMartin Pre-School case in California has made us all aware of the extent to which the very process of investigating charges of child sexual abuse can taint the legal process. Overzealous investigators may suggest things to imaginative children (who are already distraught because of the frightening nature of the investigator's questions) without intending to do so.

5. In a recent, well-publicized New York case, one of the best district attorneys in the U. S. decided not to prosecute a very vague allegation that an official in a Catholic high school had touched one of his students in an ambiguous but possibly improper way. The district attorney died suddenly, and the governor appointed a man to fill his place until the time of the next election. The interim prosecutor decided to reverse his predecessor's decision, and brought the case to trial. The tabloids avidly followed the proceedings, reporting all of the alleged victim's vague allegations that he "believed" that the school official's fingers "may have lingered for a moment" on his private parts. Predictably, the school official was acquitted. However, whereas the story of his arrest and prosecution was front-page news, the report of his acquittal was buried far back in the papers. The 3-year-long ordeal, however, has made his future as an educator uncertain.

6. Justice Oliver Wendell Holmes once offered a dramatic definition of this standard. He pictured the civil trial as an old-fashioned beam-balance scale, with weighing pans suspended from either end of the beam. He then compared the evidence to be presented to a pile of sand, with each grain of sand being a "piece" of evidence. One grain is offered as proof that the defendant did what is alleged, and it is placed on one pan; the next grain is offered as a proof that the defendant did not do what is alleged, and it is placed on the other pan. The trial proceeds in this way until all but one grain of sand has been offered, and the pans are in perfect balance. The last grain of sand, or "piece of evidence," establishes the "preponderance of the evidence" and determines the liabilities and the outcome of the trial.

7. For a recent statement of the principle, see *Evans v. Eckelman,* 265 Cal. Rptr. 605, 216 Cal. App. 3d 1609 (1st District, 1990). The Evans case cites the dissenting opinion of Judge Pearson in the Washington case of *Tyson v. Tyson,* 107 Wash. 2d 72, 727 p. 2d 226, 234–235, 55 U.S.L.W. 2273 (1986).

8. What are the possible outcomes of these contrived encounters between alleged victims and their alleged abusers? Will the one child in a thousand who is simply lying maliciously recant? Will a repentant adult break down and admit wrongdoing? In the vast majority of cases, these traumatic encounters are completely

unproductive, ending in an unresolved stand-off. In today's society, families leave such encounters convinced that the church can do nothing at all to help them, and that they must seek help elsewhere.

9. I believe it is worth noting that in the many cases on which I have worked as a consultant, fewer than 2 percent of the men involved were diagnosed as "fixated pedophiles." This simply is not a condition that significantly affects priests and religious in the U. S.

Pastoral Reflections on Child Sexual Abuse in the Church

Bishop Matthew Clark, S.T.L., J.C.L.

I have been invited to offer some pastoral reflections on child sexual abuse in the church based on my experience as a priest for twenty-seven years and as a bishop for ten.

You will understand that the invitation is one that raised mixed feelings in me when I first received it. I experienced negative feelings because the theme bespeaks pain and destruction in all who are in any way involved. It is difficult to write about the trauma of child sexual abuse that involves such deep wounds that long years of healing are usually required. Nor is it easy to write about steps to be taken toward that healing, when they can mean the shattering of lifetime dreams and the attendant public humiliation. But I do accept the invitation because I believe that all of us are called to deal with the realities in which we may find ourselves and to do that as best we can in the light of our faith. When we live our life in that light, the Spirit of God gives us strength and guidance for the journey.

Context of the Discussion
Love is a strong word in the human vocabulary. It conjures up visions of spouses responding fondly to one another, of the recip-

rocal love of parents and children, of the mutual affection of
friend for friend. It is also a strong word in the vocabulary of
Christian faith: it names God for us: "God is love." It defines our
relationships with one another in terms of Jesus's love for us:
"Love one another as I have loved you". Yet few words have been
more abused. "Love" can be trivialized, as when someone uses it
to describe a preference for a type of food or an article of clothing.
It is tragically distorted when it designates actions that are not
only devoid of love, but a repudiation of it.

In its etymology, the word "pedophilia" means "love of the
child" or "love of children." Simply in terms of its derivation, the
word should summon up thoughts of the affection of parents and,
indeed, of almost any human being for those little ones of whom
Jesus said, "Of such is the kingdom of heaven." But in a tragic
twist of language, the word pedophilia has come to mean the very
opposite of its original significance, for it speaks not of love for a
child, but of the child's sexual abuse.

As a bishop, I want to put my approach to this unhappy subject in the context of strong human and Christian love. For it is
only in such a context, and with the motivation of love, that the
various persons involved in child sexual abuse can be brought to
healing: the child first and foremost, but also the family, the offender and the community. This is not to deny that there are important legal, financial, therapeutic, educational and societal issues involved which must be dealt with firmly and honestly, as
the essays in this volume attest. It is simply to suggest the atmosphere in which these matters need to be placed if we are to have a
truly human and Christian approach to all who are involved in
the problems posed by child abuse.

Love is gentle and strong. Love is non-accusing and forgiving.
Love is soothing and healing. The many sides of Christian love
and compassion furnish the motivation and climate for a truly
pastoral approach to the issue with which we are dealing.

Closely linked to human love is human sexuality. To deal with
the sexual abuse of children in a pastoral way, we cannot isolate it
from the overall meaning of human sexuality. This abuse arises
from an illness which reveals, among other things, a warped attitude toward sexuality. Helping children, family and community
deal with the issue of sexual abuse requires a well-rounded education and training in the understanding of sexuality, its humanness, and its relationship to true human love.

Children are often afraid to speak up, even when they instinctively recognize an aberrant expression of sexuality, because many of them (though the number is decreasing) have been brought up in an atmosphere in which sexuality is not talked about. Too many parents feel ill-equipped to manage the training of their children to a well-ordered and wholesome grasp of the meaning of sexuality. Oftentimes Christian adults, fed by a culture whose moral values regarding sexuality are dubious at best, are themselves in need of a deeper appreciation of the human and Christian values that belong to God's gift of our sexuality.

The Subjects of Pastoral Concern

The Child In the 1980s there was a marked increase in the reported cases of child sexual abuse. This does not mean that it is a new problem; rather, it seems that children have been encouraged to report occurrences of sexual abuse and molestation. In addition, there are today more alert parents who are not as hesitant as the parents of earlier generations in talking to children about sexuality. Thus, it is possible for children to come forward with their stories and to do so with less guilt than in the past. I say "less guilt," because it is always difficult for children to report unseemly conduct on the part of those whom they have been taught to trust.

When a breach of that trust occurs, children are robbed of an important element in their growth toward personal security and identity. They experience betrayal from those whose role it is to help them build that security and identity. This is especially true when the offender is a priest. I remember years ago visiting a family and having dinner with them. As we sat down to eat, one of the children whispered to her mother: "Is that God?"

To children, symbols are simple and few. To see one of them broken before their eyes can have traumatic effects on faith, not just at the time, but in years to come. And psychologically, to achieve wholeness as human people, children need affirmation of their fundamental worth by those who ought to be images of human wholeness. In sexual abuse, just the opposite occurs.

More than that, children represent the future of society. What happens to them will write a history that goes beyond the possibilities of our involvement. That is why child abuse, in whatever form, poses a serious threat to the future stability of human society. This places at least two obligations on us with regard to the sexually abused child: 1) *preventive:* to do all we can, through

training, education, and legal action, to see to it that children are
protected from being thus victimized and 2) *remedial:* to offer the
necessary treatment and therapy which will begin to heal the
scars of abuse that children have suffered.

This will entail substantial financial outlays, and, with the reported incident of sexual abuse by priests, a diocese needs legal
guidance in preparing to meet such obligations. Prevention of sexual abuse and the healing of molested children represent ways of
showing a true human and Christian love toward children.

The Priest Offender Pedophilia and ephebophilia (as Dr. Lothstein's essay has suggested) are complex psychological realities
that may affect men or women, without regard to whether they
are married, single, celibate, heterosexual, or homosexual. These
disorders can affect persons who exercise leadership and influence in the community, persons normally given implicit trust because of their roles. (People are beginning to realize, however,
that being in a position of trust does not necessarily make one
trustworthy: a sad reality that can itself have destructive effects
on the commonweal.)

There seems to be serious evidence that many child sex abusers, pedophiles and ephebophiles, were themselves molested in
childhood. One of the responsibilities the church has, for the good
of society, the church, and the priest offender, is to see to it that
the offender receives effective support and treatment to enable
him or her to deal with his illness.

Does this suggest that there should be, in a diocese, trained
psychologists or psychiatrists, perhaps priests trained in these dis-
ciplines, who could offer the kind of support and clinical help that
is needed? Is this an activity that belongs to the diocesan office of
"Ministry to Priests"? I know from my reading and experience
that child sexual abuse arises from a disorder that is complex and
that even experts do not know all that is to be known about this
phenomenon.

I do not exclude the possibility that there may be subjective
guilt attached to such activity which clearly is damaging to so
many. But I do consider it more realistic to think of the priest who
is an abuser as an afflicted person rather than as a sinner, as one
who needs healing and support rather than condemnation.

Two realities lead me to that disposition.

The first is the widespread damage that is done. It is hard for me to conceive of any priest who could possibly want to inflict such enormous damage on so many innocent people. He damages his victims, and thus their healing should be the focus of any pastoral response. But he also causes possible irreparable damage to himself. And clearly he wounds his brother priests, the particular faith community in which he serves, and the community at large. Given all of this, it is difficult to imagine that one would freely choose a line of conduct which could result in such devastation to oneself and to so many other persons. I can get a better grasp on the reality when I understand such conduct to be born of an illness and/or addiction which so limits the understanding or freedom of the person as to make such conduct somehow attractive or desirable—or uncontrollable.

The second reality is the abusive priests' perceived incapacity to recognize and come to grips with the grave damage they cause. I have heard of some who express regret "for any *inconvenience* they have caused" but who cannot articulate a recognition that their conduct has produced damage, pain, and anger. Further evidence of this is their belief that they can resume a normal relationship with their victims and their victims' families.

When such a limited sense of reality or proportion is evident, it seems a much more profitable path to presume that the abuser is ill. This does not exclude the possibility that he is subjectively guilty of sin. Such a determination, however, is between the individual and God. This presumption of illness allows all parties concerned to begin to deal as constructively as possible with the terrible effects of child abuse in those victimized. And it gives some hope to the abuser that, although he must bear the very strong consequences of his actions, he will not be cast out and abandoned by the community.

Elements of a Pastoral Response

What are some guides we can use in order to respond in a pastoral way to this most difficult situation? I suggest the following elements for consideration.

1. *Anyone who raises a complaint of child sexual abuse about a priest has a right to be heard and should be heard as soon as reasonably possible.* If the party making the allegation wishes to take it to the bishop, the bishop is well-advised to receive the party himself. I would recommend that the bishop have the company of an advisor who can serve as a witness to the conversation. The presence of

such a person provides several benefits. In addition to being a witness to the conversation, such a person can help the bishop reflect upon the content of the conversation, and be of assistance in developing appropriate follow-up to it.

It is important to elicit the facts in as much detail as possible. I think it is also important to keep notes of such conversations and, at the end of the meeting, to review the notes so that all can comment on their accuracy.

Because meetings of this kind can be emotionally charged for everyone involved, it is important to do everything possible to create an environment in which all parties can be as peaceful and as open as possible. The bishop can contribute to this by receiving warmly the person(s) making the allegations and listening carefully and respectfully to what they say.

After hearing the allegations, the bishop might ask questions which, in his judgment, would help clarify the nature and circumstances of the alleged wrongdoing. I would include here questions which would provide a fuller understanding of the allegation and/or relate to apparent inconsistencies in it. Again, I recommend that there be no appearance of attacking the story. I would tell the parties involved that I would follow up the interview by speaking with the priest charged with misconduct and that I would communicate with them about that conversation as soon as reasonably possible.

2. *The priest accused of sexual abuse of a minor has a right to know his accuser and the charge made against him, and he has the right to defend himself.* Complaints against leaders in the community, in general, and against priests, in particular, are not uncommon. In my years as a bishop and in earlier ministries, I have received many of them. Some have related to serious matters; others concern trivial things. Some charges are made in a responsible manner; others seem to be made frivolously. Unless the charges are patently frivolous and trivial, the priest charged has a right to know them and to respond to them. And when the charge relates to the sexual abuse of a minor or to other matters of comparable gravity, it is my opinion that the priest has a right to know that the charge was made, even if by all appearances, it was made frivolously. His right to protect his reputation entitles him to that awareness. That is especially true when he is subject to the exposure in the mass media. The gravity of the charge, its volatile nature in the community, and the vulnerability of the one charged in the public arena

entitles him, I believe, to all of the support I can offer to him. And however painful the sharing of the charge may be for all concerned, I believe that the protection of the priest and the common good demand that this sharing occur.

The communication by a bishop to a priest of an accusation of serious misconduct is a painful experience for both persons, most especially for the priest. But if it is done with sensitivity and in an environment which bespeaks respect and support, it can, notwithstanding all of the pain it may entail, be a constructive step.

In the interview, the priest should be reassured that its purpose is to share with him as fully as possible a complaint that has been made against him. I would want to say to him that the interview is meant to honor both the rights to be heard of the person making the allegations and the priest's right to know his accuser and the allegations being made against him. He, of course, has the right to ask any questions or make any observations he wishes.

Possibly, his response will indicate that the accusation made against him is without warrant. If the evidence indicates that the accusation is indeed without foundation, I would recommend another meeting with the accusing parties to share those findings. If, in the face of the evidence developed to that point, they choose to withdraw, the matter is finished. If they dispute the material presented I would meet again with the accused priest and continue searching for the truth, which often surfaces rather quickly. The bishop should have knowledge of a professional counselor who can offer assistance even during this process of surfacing the truth.

If the priest admits to the allegations made against him, I would suspend him immediately from his ministerial assignment. I would then enlist the support of a team of qualified persons to develop a program to help the individual take responsibility for his actions and to foster his healing and rehabilitation.

If the priest denies the allegation, but there is some evidence that the allegation is credible, I would remove him from his assignment until such time as the matter could be clarified. Naturally, this clarification should be sought as soon as reasonably possible. I am aware that this removal is a severe step and that, at first glance, it could be seen as a harsh and unwarranted decision. Indeed, as we worked on policies governing such issues for our diocese, I had a similar concern. I will not go into the details of that discussion here, except to say that the step is designed to protect the priest, the bishop, and the faith community from accusations of insufficient care for the well-being of possible victims of sexual abuse.

3. *Victims of child abuse are entitled to all the support the community can reasonably offer.* I would judge that this support would begin with a proper evaluation, by professionals, of the abused children, and the formulation and financing of a program designed to heal the traumas they experienced. It may well be that the nature and circumstances of the victims' families would warrant a similar response to them.

4. *In the ideal order, a priest who is a child molester could come through treatment to a level of personal integration that would allow him to resume his public ministry in a peaceful and fruitful way.* In that same ideal order, people who were aware of the priest's past problems would recognize his healing and welcome him back in their midst with confidence.

In my opinion, that ideal order does not yet exist. Our society is so litigious, the potential for harm so great, and the liabilities so severe that it is difficult for me to imagine circumstances in which I would assign a priest publicly known to have a history of child sexual abuse to minister in our diocese or allow him to do so in any other diocese.

Exceptions might be made, as clinical and therapeutic expertise advances. But in the present climate, so prone to litigation and sensationalism, all parties may be well-served by the priest not returning to pastoral ministry. Differing perspectives are emerging on this point, certainly indicating that such decisions must be made most carefully and in consultation with treatment and legal experts.

5. *The priest who is a child molester deserves every support the bishop and community can reasonably give.* This priest should never be made or allowed to feel outside the care of the community. At times, the parents of victimized children can possess remarkable levels of understanding and compassion for the abuser. They want the abuser held accountable but speak more of personal healing than of punishment for him. At other times, enraged relatives of the victims will consider their children to have been destroyed by the priest and will insist that he, in turn, should be destroyed. The attitude of the relatives of the victims will be a significant factor in the shaping of a program which holds the abuser responsible for his actions but also allows for healing and greater freedom for all involved.

The Presbyterate
There is a need to train priests so that they can understand this illness and recognize it where it exists. Obviously this does not mean priests "spying" on priests, but it does mean priests being concerned for the welfare of fellow priests, the good of society and the church, and most especially for the well-being of our children. I would recommend clergy conferences on sexuality conducted by trained personnel where this issue would be discussed and placed in context. Also, there is a need for legal counsel, making clear to the entire presbyterate the considerable financial and legal responsibilities that could well be incurred when priests are convicted of child abuse.

The Family of the Child
The bishop has a responsibility not only to the children, the priest-offender and the presbyterate, but also to the families of the abused children. As mentioned earlier, their dispositions may run the gamut from bewilderment to belligerence. The warmth of Christian love and compassion must be extended to them. They must be assured that the priest will be "disciplined" in a way that will prevent future occurrences of child abuse. They need, too, the assurance for the children and for themselves of the necessary therapy to help heal the wounds they have experienced.

The Community
How should the local church respond to its own members, both the community of the local church and to the larger community, when such a crisis occurs? *It is neither desirable nor possible to suppress, deny, or ignore what has actually happened.* An honest news report is necessary. It should make clear that positive steps are being taken to deal with the situation in its entirety. Such a report has to be written with care and with proper legal advice. (See Carol Stanton's essay for practical suggestions concerning a public response.)

A diocese needs to be prepared for such an eventuality. Writing such a report, one has to take into consideration the effect it will have on all parties concerned. Does this call for someone who can represent the diocese and who will be well-informed on the psychological and social aspects of pedophilia and ephebophilia? The situation is too sensitive to be entrusted to amateurs. Wanting to act in love and compassion does not preclude acting in a professional way that will be respected by professionals.

One of the important aspects of dealing with the community is preserving the credibility of the church. Honesty in admitting culpability and accepting responsibility for remedial care, and absolute refusal to hide the facts, will be ways of admitting to the humanness of the church, in its goodness and in its sinfulness. *The church is never hurt by admitting its humanity; it is often hurt by pretending to deny it or to excuse it.*

Priests who are pedophiles or ephebophiles have caused great damage (as the two anonymous contributors to this volume poignantly demonstrate). They harm their victims, their victims' families, and themselves. In addition, they cause harm to their brother priests and to the community at large.

I do not have any ready solutions to the problem. I do believe that the situation whenever or wherever it may arise must be dealt with directly and honestly. First and foremost, the abused child must be cared for; every effort must be made to heal the damage that has been done. Secondly, a similar concern must be shown to family members of the abused child. Thirdly, the priest who is guilty of such conduct must take responsibility for his actions and their consequences. He should not be left alone to do this but rather should experience the support of his bishop and other friends in the community.

The Spirit of God gives us strength and guidance for the journey. But these gifts do not undo the harm that has been done. Nor do they provide quick and painless solutions. But they do help us to be loving and compassionate. When we can offer those gifts, even in the most painful of circumstances, then we bear witness in a powerful way to much that is central to our Christian faith: that God's love is faithful and enduring; that no sister or brother should ever be excluded from the care of the community; and that love is a choice which is often painful but always life-giving.

A Challenge to the People of God

Rev. Stephen J. Rossetti, D.Min.

The sexual abuse of children is a devastating event for all involved. The perpetrators become marked persons who must suffer the ridicule and disdain of an entire society, as well as the more punishing reproach that they often inflict upon themselves. The damage caused to the victims is equally severe. They may suffer from bouts of depression, anxiety, uncontrollable fears, suicidal thoughts, or eating disorders. Worse yet, in an effort to master the terrible trauma that eats away within their souls, they may themselves become abusers.

The damage it has caused, and will continue to cause, our community of faith is also great. This is hard to accept because the numbers involved are so few. It has taken hundreds of years and countless hours of selfless devotion to build up a family of faith centered upon a bond of trust. Can this family be destroyed so quickly by so few? It is one of the most serious scandals that the church has ever had to face because it destroys the one element that is essential for ministry: trust.

We, the people of God, may be tempted to look at the sexual abuse of children as though we were spectators, and label the child sexual abuser as "someone not like us." Thus, we might believe that our only goal is to rid ourselves of such men either by expelling them from our midst or treating them in psychological facilities until they change.

But is such an approach enough? Does the existence of child molesters mean only that there are a few sick men and women in our otherwise healthy society? It may be that the roots of the problem are much deeper and more extensive than first blush would reveal. It may be that providing treatment for abusers and their victims is only addressing what psychology names the "presenting" problem.

For example, when someone enters psychotherapy, he or she begins with a "presenting problem." This initial problem is usually one of a variety of distressing symptoms such as anxiety, compulsive behavior, irrational fears, or simply feeling "down." The client hopes that the psychologist can help get rid of this symptom. The psychologist, however, will look at this symptom not as the core of the real problem, but merely as an indicator of an underlying conflict of which the person is unaware. One of the tasks of psychodynamic therapy is to help the client take his or her gaze off the symptom and to refocus on the underlying conflict.

It might be illuminating to view the phenomenon of child sexual abuse not as the entire problem, but merely as a symptom of an underlying problem in our society of which we are not fully aware. Perhaps the challenge we face and the tasks that lie ahead are more extensive and fundamental than merely the treatment of the immediate effects of the sexual abuse. The questions then arise: *Where* do we look for the more fundamental problems? *What* is the nature of these problems?

Where Do We Look?

Thomas Merton, Trappist monk and writer, entitled one of his books *Conjectures of a Guilty Bystander*. Even as a monk, and later a hermit, Merton felt connected to and part of the larger society. His years of meditation and reflection brought him to the point where he sensed that he was partially "responsible" not only for the successes of the world, but also for its ills. Merton liked to quote from poet John Donne: "No man is an island entire of itself; every man is a piece of the continent, a part of the main." If we were to use Merton's spiritual perspective, we might look for the locus of the problem, not outside of ourselves or in another place. Rather, his approach indicates that we should look for the core of the problem within our own hearts.

Using a family approach would yield a similar perspective. For example, when family members bring in one of its members for treatment, they often believe that this "identified patient" is the only sick person. They have tacitly agreed that all the rest of them are healthy. A family counselor would try to help them become aware that the entire system is dysfunctional and that all the members contribute, in some way, to the patient's disorder. It is not surprising that such efforts are sometimes met with surprise, denial and/or anger. But for the counselor, the identified patient is only a symptom of a larger dysfunction. To enable the system to become healthier, the counselor believes that everyone in the family has to change.

In the same way, we might look at the problem of child sexual abuse from a family perspective. Using this approach, we would see ourselves as a family in which one of the members has been discovered to be afflicted with the illness of pedophilia or ephebophilia. While the identified patient is truly ill and needs treatment, a family approach would locate the underlying source of the illness within the entire family. *The existence of pedophilia and ephebophilia might be seen as a symptom of an underlying disorder within our entire society.*

However, one might wonder how anyone, even someone espousing a family perspective, could possibly link such serious pathology as pedophilia with "normal" people like us. At first glance, it would appear that we, the pedophiles' "family," have nothing in common with them or their illness.

But, have you ever read a psychology textbook that described different mental illnesses? The first time you do this, it might be a bit disconcerting. The author will describe the downcast mood of depression, the compulsive behavior that accompanies an obsession, the idiosyncratic behavior of schizophrenia, and the self-centered focus of narcissism. A frightening thought comes to mind when these symptoms are first described, "Oh no, I do this. Yes, I do that, too. My gosh, I am a neurotic mess. I have all these disorders." The truth is, you are right; you *do* have them all.

When you walk out of the house, do you check the door that one extra time to make sure it is locked? You know it is foolish; you know you just locked it, but you want to check just to make yourself feel better. In a similar vein, we are all sometimes afflicted with fears and anxieties about insignificant things. We become tense even when we realize there is no logical reason to be afraid. And occasionally, we become downcast and lose our energy and zest for life. Perhaps we lose our appetites or have difficulty sleeping. When we wake up in the morning, we still feel tired and do not want to get out of bed.

This is the stuff of which pathology is born. It is the obsessive-compulsive who is filled with anxiety until he or she checks the door that one last time. The "anxiety neurotic" feels an unreasonable fear. And it is the depressed person who loses energy and vitality. He or she is the one who may wake up tired and feel as if an enormous dead weight is being dragged through life.

Certainly, there is a significant difference between the truly mentally ill person and ourselves. The one who is clinically diagnosed an obsessive-compulsive will check the door so many times that it interferes with his or her life. This person may spend hours checking or arranging things in a particular order to reduce anxiety. The anxiety neurotic may be so frightened about going outside that he or she is confined to the prison of the home (agoraphobia). A diagnosable depression will be severe enough to affect a person's entire perception of life and throw it into such a negative cast that it seriously impairs the possibility of a productive life. However, the "seeds" of such disorders are found in all of us.

Could it not be that the seeds of pedophilia and ephebophilia are likewise found in us? Perhaps the sexual perversion found in the child molester has echoes within ourselves. Robert Stoller has studied the dynamics of sexual excitement in both perverse and "normal" people. At one point in his career, he attempted to distinguish clearly between perversion and a normal pattern of arousal. He finally concluded that such a clear distinction did not exist. He stated: "I came to these conclusions as I sought and failed to find, as many others also had failed (e.g., Freud), a line on the continuum of sexual behavior that could separate normal from perverse (Stoller, 1976).

Stoller summarized his findings by saying that the dynamics of sexual excitement found in a perversion (including mystery, risk, illusion, revenge, reversal of trauma, safety factors, dehumanization, and *hostility*) are also found in the sexual excitement of the general population. It is not surprising that Stoller's ideas, like the counselor's suggestions to a family that they all share in the illness of the sick person, have been met with some resistance.

But if Stoller is correct, then we have much more in common with the pedophile and the ephebophile than we might have initially guessed. Thus, the family perspective cited earlier might indeed be appropriate. It may be that the identified patient—the child molester—represents an underlying disorder in our wider society and in our entire community of faith. Though we may not personally be the ones who molest children, pedophilia and ephebophilia can be thought of as illnesses that spring from the context of our family. It is our entire family that is ill and is in need of healing.

What, then, is our illness? What specifically is the family context that enables the illnesses of pedophilia and ephebophilia to emerge? If we are able to identify some of the underlying disorders in our society that give rise to child sexual abuse, it might challenge us all to change.

What Are the Underlying Disorders?

First of all, the existence of sexual perversions in our family indicates that our understanding and appropriation of sexual impulses and sexual desires are flawed. When one looks at the portrayal of sexuality in our culture, it would not be unfair to call it an obsession. One who is obsessed with something is preoccupied. It becomes a persistent idea or desire that cannot be expelled. Our preoccupation with sex has become so pervasive that sex has become a medium of exchange. It sells products. It determines one's worth. It is bartered for favors and position. It is truly an obsession.

Patrick Carnes, author of *Out of the Shadows* and pioneer in the treatment of sexual problems, has summarized his clinical findings with respect to the cause and treatment of sexual obsessions. He has come to call these sexual problems "addictions," because they function much like more well-known addictions to alcohol and other substances. The perpetrator of child sexual abuse is often, like the alcoholic, out of control, obsessed with desire, and driven to find satisfaction. As the alcoholic reacts to alcohol, so does the child abuser react to sexual encounters with children.

Carnes says that several core beliefs underlie the sex addict's view of the world. These faulty beliefs give rise to and fuel his addiction. Core Belief 1: "I am basically a bad, unworthy person." The sex addict feels inadequate and believes himself or herself to be a failure. Core Belief 2: "No one would love me as I am." The addict feels unlovable by others, and thus isolated. Core Belief 3: "My needs are never going to be met if I have to depend on others." Addicts cannot reach out to others for help, so they may become resentful, self-pitying, depressed, and even suicidal. Core

Belief 4: "Sex is my most important need." The sex addict confuses love, warmth, and affirmation with sex (Carnes, 1983).

Feelings of inadequacy (Belief 1), being unlovable (Belief 2), and feeling emotionally isolated (Belief 3) are widespread in our society. Such distorted beliefs facilitate and sustain our obsession with sexuality. In addition, there are signs everywhere that we confuse love, warmth and affirmation with sex. It appears that sex has become our most important need (Belief 4).

When sexuality becomes an obsession in the family, one should not be surprised when a sexual perversion subsequently arises. Good seed and good soil produce good fruit. Bad seed and bad soil produce bad fruit.

Is Our Community of Faith Any Different?

One would hope and pray that our community of faith would be different from our society. If society is obsessed with sex, we would want our community of believers to be different. We would want ourselves to model a healthier understanding of human sexuality and to place it in a more modest perspective, while not denying its power and its creative potential. We should be a "sign of contradiction." Unfortunately, this may not be the case.

For example, a parishioner was criticizing the beliefs of a certain person. She said, "This person is not a true Catholic. He does not believe the *central* teachings of our faith." When asked to explain she said, "He does not accept our teaching on birth control, masturbation, homosexuality, and premarital sex." While our church teaches clearly about these matters, they are hardly the *central* teachings of our faith. One might consider other truths to be more essential, such as: God is one; Jesus alone is Lord and Savior; He has died and He is risen.

Often, the battle lines between liberals and conservatives are drawn around these "central" teachings on human sexuality. Theologians and faithful alike are labeled based on their positions on these subjects. There is so much energy put into defending these teachings of the ordinary magisterium of the church, one would be tempted to say that we, too, are obsessed with sexuality. Would that such energy and commitment were used in proclaiming that the Reign of God is at hand! But, our community of faith, too, arises out of a societal context. It is hard for us to be different from the society at large.

Perusing the New Testament, one finds few, if any, original

teachings of Jesus that speak directly about human sexuality. He spoke about the sanctity of marriage. He held up celibacy "for the sake of the Kingdom." However, human sexuality appears not to have been a major focus of his teaching. The closest parable might be found in John 8: the woman caught in the act of adultery. She had, indeed, committed a sexual sin. However, the point of the story is not the gravity of her sin, though Jesus does not deny that it was, in fact, a sin. Rather, the parable drives home the reality of compassion and forgiveness, something that had been forgotten in the religious climate in which Jesus lived. How have we come to place so much emphasis on something that Jesus spoke of so rarely?

At the same time that we are *obsessed* with the sexual conduct of others and its moral consequences, we often *repress* our own internal sexual impulses. Instead of sexual feelings becoming the focus of our thoughts and actions as in an obsession, they are put out of consciousness altogether. When this repression occurs, it is because our sexual desires are unwanted, unacceptable, and thought to be unholy. While repression initially appears to be a safer course of action than an obsession, especially for the vowed religious, the end result may be equally deadly.

I remember asking one of the therapists at a residential treatment program for priests and religious what the most common ailment was that brought these people to such an emotional state that residential psychological care was needed. She replied, "We get the good ones." She went on to explain that sisters, brothers and priests who tried to be so good and so holy for many years sometimes lost a sense of their own selves with all their needs and desires. They lost a sense of the importance of their need as men and women for warmth and affection. They were buried under a Roman collar or a habit, and under a false understanding of holiness. They forgot they were human.

This dehumanization is often reinforced by those we serve. A priest recently related an incident concerning his eighth-grade religious education class. One of the students very honestly asked him, "Do priests get erections?" In a similar incident, during my first week at the parish, a little girl innocently asked me, "Do priests go to the bathroom?" Every priest and sister can think of similar incidents. Such questions are perennial.

Even in this post-Vatican II "enlightened" era, there is a subtle belief that to be a priest or religious is to be different. To make a public commitment to a religious life and the path of Christian holiness is thought to be "different," and this state of being "different" is usually translated by lay people to mean "not like me." And "not like me" means not having elimination needs, sexual impulses, or a real humanity.

Such misconceptions within dedicated Christians can spawn a repression of, or an obsession with, sexual desires. They may subtly turn priests and religious into rigid tin soldiers or driven, guilt-ridden slaves. When the errors become more pronounced, they can facilitate a variety of distressing symptoms such as anxieties, compulsive behavior, or even pedophilia.

Sexually deviant behaviors do not arise from a society, a community of faith, and a family that have a healthy understanding of human sexuality. They spring from a climate of repression and/ or obsession. But pedophilia, ephebophilia, and other sexually deviant behaviors are not only crimes stemming from a perverse sexuality. They require another, equally important societal illness in order to thrive. There is another human impulse, in addition to human sexuality, which is equally powerful, equally unwanted, and thought to be equally unholy. There is an integral connection between human aggression and child sexual abuse.

Human Aggression and Child Abuse

Robert Stoller (1975) published an important work on deviant sexual behavior entitled *Perversion: The Erotic Form of Hatred*. His primary thesis is contained in the title: Sexual perversions stem from an inner hatred which has somehow become eroticized. Thus, rape, voyeurism, exhibitionism, and the many forms that sexual perversions can take are actually acts of hostility that witness to an underlying rage in the soul of the perpetrator.

The actual vehicle by which this internal hatred has become eroticized remains a mystery. However, Stoller says that clues may be found in one's sexual fantasies. These fantasies develop as a result of one's childhood and adolescent experiences in the real world. Society and family heap upon the future sex offender painful experiences, traumatic events, and distorted beliefs. The resulting sexual fantasies and subsequent deviant sexual behavior invariably include aggression. As Stoller says, "And at the center is hostility."

Child molesters cringe from such understandings of their behavior. They object to any hint that their actions may have been aggressive or hostile. They may say, "I loved the child." "I was his best friend." "It was an act of nurturing." Indeed, the sexual abuse of children is usually performed quietly with little, if any, display of force. It appears as a gentle, mutually consenting act.

This is the lie of the sexual abuse of children. The seduction is insidious. The violence is covert. The children are emotionally coerced by more powerful adults in whom they trust and to whom they commit themselves. And to keep the seduction covert, the victims are almost imperceptibly pressured into remaining silent: "If you tell, I will get into trouble. You do not want me to get into trouble, do you?" Or even more insidiously done, the molesters may suggest, "This is our secret because you and I are friends." Thus, the truth is not only kept from the outside world, it is hidden from the victims and the perpetrators as well.

Underneath this lie of "mutual consent" is the truth that an enormously hostile and violent act is being done to a young child. While the perpetrator may strenuously disagree, the results of this "loving" act bear witness to the truth. The child is emotionally scarred. The family is damaged. Society is shocked and the community of faith is wounded. The Scriptures tell us, "By their fruits you shall know them." The fruits of this "loving" act are so destructive, they can only be the result of a violent deed.

Stoller notes that most sexual deviants are male. It is true that aggressive impulses are present in both the male and the female; these impulses must be acknowledged and managed by both sexes. However, I would hypothesize that it is especially important for the male to accept and integrate these aggressive impulses in order to achieve a masculine identity. This is not to say that males are aggressive and females are not. Rather, it is to suggest that to be male in our modern world necessitates a fundamental connection with human aggression. Such a connection may be something innate to the male gender or it may be a learned societal role. Nonetheless, if he does not come to terms with his aggressive impulses, he will have difficulty developing a masculine identity and he will either become violent, or emasculated, or both.

It is not surprising, then, that child molesters usually have a difficult time managing their emotions, especially their aggressive and hostile feelings. One psychiatrist said that child molesters often have an "inadequate personality." Other clinicians will stress the molesters' "tenuous masculine identity" and point out that they feel weak and childish around other adults. Child molesters tend to be *emasculated* in that they repress their aggressive selves and appear to be powerless. But they are also *violent* in their act of sexually abusing children.

Child sexual abuse is not only a failure to integrate one's sexual desires and needs, it is also a failure to integrate one's aggressive impulses.

Human Aggression and Our Community of Faith

Once again, the pathology of the pedophile and ephebophile does not arise in a vacuum. It is spawned in a society and in a climate that enables it to arise and to thrive. Let us look at the two extremes, obsession and repression, and see if our society and our community of faith may be a seedbed of such illnesses.

Like its obsession with sexuality, we note in our society a dismal attempt to achieve a healthy appropriation of human aggression. There appears to be a rising amount of overt violence such as armed conflicts, murders, terrorism, rapes and family violence. More subtle forms of violence appear no less prevalent including racism, sexism, coercion, subtle threats, pornography, and child sex abuse. We are living in one of the most violent eras of human history. One could easily make a case for our society being on the verge of an obsession with violence.

Again, we hope that our community of faith would be a sign of contradiction to a violent world. However, we acknowledge that this community emerges from a society obsessed with violence and it is unlikely to be radically different. Just as our society shows indications that it is driven by human violence, our community of faith also manifests signs of an inability to manage human aggression.

To illustrate, a priest related an incident when he was a pastor in a parish. The rectory housekeeper answered the door to greet one of the many street people who showed up asking for assistance. After she opened the door, a conversation ensued in which the street person was becoming increasingly belligerent and abusive. Being the timid sort, the housekeeper just stood there, almost paralyzed with fear. Whereupon the pastor walked to the door and, as the street person acknowledged, with "fire in his eyes," stopped the abuse. At that point, the abuser objected, "You're a priest; you're supposed to be nice."

One would guess that, for many in our community of faith, a "nice" priest would speak kindly in all situations. He would be soft-spoken and never raise his voice. He might remind us of the image of priesthood portrayed in the television show M.A.S.H. "Father Mulcahey" was kind, quiet, and unassuming. However, he appeared to be a largely ineffectual man who seemed weak and insignificant. Such "nice" priests may fit our preconceived notion of holiness, but the fact is they are dehumanized. It is likely that their aggressive impulses have been repressed.

In the October 7, 1989 issue of *America* magazine, Patrick M. Arnold wrote a controversial essay, "In Search of the Hero," in which he postulated that there is an anti-masculine sexism in our community of faith. He said there are "subtly hostile attitudes toward men and maleness." He believed that males in our church are being emasculated.

It was an explosive issue and the editors received many letters in response. While one might not agree with everything that Arnold says, it is important to consider his fundamental thesis that maleness is being caricatured today as being rigid, violent, domineering, power-hungry and oppressive. He admits, "No doubt this is because women have suffered so much under the 'shadow' of static or rigid maleness: unbending laws...and oppressive violence." In both this caricature of male violence and the resulting emasculated male, one sees an obsession with, and then a repression of, the impulse of aggression.

In former days, people accused an essentially male-dominated hierarchy of control, competition for power, rigid enforcement of laws, and dominating behavior. Whenever this occurred, and I do not say such behavior was always the case, it was an act of violence and a failure to manage human aggression properly. Such subtle forms of violence are no more authentically male, or human, than the disguised aggression of the child sex molester.

Today, if Arnold is correct, the pendulum has swung to the other extreme. Men are apologizing for being male. They see their own male drives toward independence, strength and truth as being somehow flawed or bad. Men may be receiving a subtle message that it is not okay for them to have a strong intellect; it is not okay for them to speak the truth fearlessly; and it is not okay to disagree.

And the God of our faith is becoming emasculated as well. Yahweh is allowed to be kind, forgiving, and compassionate; Yahweh, in this perception, would never discipline the people, nor could anyone possibly end up in hell.

But both dominating behavior (obsession with aggression) and emasculation (repression of aggression) are pathological and hinder the development of the true male identity and the successful integration of human aggression. Once again, we might blame a pre-Vatican II mentality of being anti-human and thus responsible for this aberration. But I suspect that such maldevelopments are not unique to our era. Like our ageless, distorted belief that to be holy is to be asexual, I suspect we have always been tempted, under the guise of holiness, to believe that anger and other "negative" emotions have no place in the Kingdom of God.

To be authentically Christian, however, the emotional power and strength of one's aggression must be felt, contained, and channeled appropriately. Jesus was not "nice." He fashioned a whip and cleansed the temple; he screamed at the Scribes and Pharisees, calling them "hypocrites," "whitened sepulchers," "fools," and "blind guides." Jesus "looked around at them with anger" (Mark 3:5). Jesus was not emasculated.

On the other hand, this powerful Jesus did not appear controlling. He enticed people to believe. He encouraged them with signs of his love. And although he challenged their mistaken ideas, he never forced them. Jesus left them free to choose. He even allowed Judas to betray him: "Be quick about what you are to do" (John 13:27). What the child abuser lacks, and what the community of faith strives for, we see realized in the person of Jesus.

Our Challenge
The challenge to our community is to value, yet to place in perspective, the human impulses of aggression and sexuality.

Pedophilia and ephebophilia do not exist in a society that has fully integrated its humanity. Though we may not be individually guilty of the crime of child sexual abuse, as a community we are not only responsible for the good that springs from our midst, we are also responsible for the evil as well. We are the seedbed from which such pathology is born. We are, like Merton, guilty bystanders.

The belief "To be holy is not to be human" is a tenacious falsehood and its presence is likely to span the history of our religion. It is more pervasive than Jansenism or philosophical dualism. It is more timeless than the pre-Vatican II Thomistic era. I suspect it has something to do with the serpent and the original sin of humanity. Perhaps it is the evil one who would have us believe that we are disembodied gods.

To struggle with the vicissitudes of our human impulses is an inescapable part of the Christian life. As we struggle to integrate our aggression and sexuality, we are to strike the middle of the balance. We are to be neither repressed nor obsessed. We are neither dehumanized nor are we driven by our impulses. Perhaps the best word to describe this mid-point is freedom. The Christian is not a slave to human drives, but orders them in service of a higher human calling.

To integrate our aggressive selves, we are to be strong without being controlling or power-hungry. We are to speak the truth without being dogmatic or legalistic. We are to be assertive without being aggressive or destructive. And we are to be independent without being cold or distant.

In a similar way, to be a fully free sexual person, we are called to be warm, compassionate, intimate and engaged. We find delight in others. Yet, we are not manipulating, seductive, or sterile. Nor do we use others or dehumanize them to gratify our own sexual desires.

These are difficult tasks to accomplish. Integrating one's sexuality and aggression have been a perennial problem in the Christian life. Even in the sixteenth century, Hieronymus Bosch, the Dutch painter, complained that religion fostered a repression of sexuality and aggression. In his paintings, he depicted the church as repressing these desires in the name of holiness (Kaufmann, 1989).

While psychology may help us to understand the tasks that lie ahead and to begin the treatment, the human sciences are powerless to complete the necessary human transformation. Psychology, by itself, would leave us with a pessimistic view: We can only try to integrate our sexual and aggressive selves. We may understand the goal with our heads, but our hearts lag far behind. Perhaps we will never fully integrate our sexual and aggressive selves; it may be that such a task will always remain undone and incomplete.

While we may have to accept this incompleteness, we must nevertheless take responsibility for our behavior and its ramifications. Our society will be replete with violence, overt and covert. We will be driven by our sexual and aggressive impulses, and our society will use sex as its medium of exchange and violence for its entertainment. And there will be men and women who will dehumanize others—even children—and use them as sexual objects.

Our faith will not spare us from these terrible results of our weaknesses and sins. Nor will it allow us to bypass the important insights and recommendations of the secular sciences in treating our illnesses. But the true sign of hope and final cure is found in the humanity of Jesus. It was a humanity that identified with our weaknesses and carried these frailties through the hopelessness of death into the new life of the resurrection.

It has been my hope that we, like Jesus, would identify with the weaknesses of our humanity, especially in one of its most crippled forms—the pedophile. Truly, we are not unlike the pedophile. To separate this person from us is to perpetuate the unintegrated state of our society. In such a separation, we maintain a mask of civility and sanity much like the Pharisee who prayed, "I give you thanks, O God, that I am not like the rest of men—grasping, crooked, adulterous" (Luke 18:11). It was not this Pharisee who went home in peace.

In reality, the Pharisee and all of us are "like the rest of men." If we sense an uncomfortable familiarity with the child molester, it is because there is something dark within ourselves that understands this evil. If we have come to identify with the child molester, it is because he or she is a member of our family. And if his or her struggles are much like our struggles, it is because our task is the same. Our prayer in the face of the sexual abuse of children can only be the prayer of the tax collector, "O God, be merciful to me, a sinner" (Luke 18:13).

The power of the resurrection does not flow fully through us when we profess our wholeness and sinlessness. It comes to us after an experience of the weakness of our humanity—a humanity that is fated to the ultimate weakness and final humiliation of dying. Our society, and our community of faith, have been attempting to face courageously the evil of child sexual abuse in our families. It is a difficult and disturbing task. It has caused us to die a little.

To engage ourselves in this task truly causes us to die a little. We are forced to face a terrible evil in our community of faith and to see the weaknesses of our own family. It also invites us to look at ourselves and to recognize the brokenness that lies within. As we face the weaknesses incumbent upon our humanity, we come, paradoxically, to know the freedom and the peace of the resurrection.

This may be the hardest yet potentially the most liberating

challenge the child molester places before us: to see within ourselves the seeds of this tragedy, and to recognize in the face of the
perpetrator the features of our own countenance.

References

Arnold, Patrick M. "In Search of the Hero: Masculine Spirituality and Liberal Christianity." *America.* 161:9 (October 7, 1989): 206–
210.

Carnes, Patrick. *Out of the Shadows: Understanding Sexual Addiction.* Minneapolis: CompCare Publishers, 1983.

Kaufmann, Yoram. "Analytical Psychotherapy." In *Current Psy-
chotherapies*, edited by Raymond J. Corsini and Danny Wedding.
Itasca, Illinois: F.E. Peacock Pubs. Inc., 1989, pp. 119–152.

Stoller, Robert J. *Perversion: The Erotic Form of Hatred.* Washington, D.C.: American Psychiatric Press, Inc., 1975.

_____ . "Sexual Excitement." *Archives of General Psychiatry.* August, 1976, 33:899–909.

Key Terms

Pedophile: an adult who has recurrent intense, sexual urges and sexually arousing fantasies involving sexual activity with a prepubescent child. The age of the child is arbitrarily set at thirteen years or younger and the adult is at least five years older than the child.

Ephebophile: an adult who has recurrent intense, sexual urges, and sexually arousing fantasies involving sexual activity with a pubescent child or adolescent through the age of seventeen. The youngest age of the child is arbitrarily set at fourteen years and the adult is at least five years older than the child.

Paraphilia: the attraction for something beyond the norm. A term which replaced "perversion" because of the latter's pejorative connotations. In psychiatric jargon, the term paraphilia designates the entire class of variant sexual behaviors that were previously called deviant or perverse.

The Authors

Mollie Brown, RSM, is a psychiatric nurse and holds a Ph.D. in human development from the University of Chicago. She is the Founding and Executive Director of Spirit House Therapeutic Community, a primary prevention resource for women religious. She maintains a clinical practice, serving religious, clergy, and laity. She does workshops in the areas of formation, gerontology and related issues. Mollie Brown can be contacted at Spirit House, Inc., 72 Dorvid Road, Rochester, NY 14617.

Bishop Matthew Clark graduated from the North American College and was ordained in Rome in 1962. He holds both a S.T.L. and J.C.L. from the Gregorian. After a variety of assignments in his native diocese of Albany, New York, he returned to Rome as a spiritual director of the North American College. In 1979, he was ordained bishop by Pope John II for the Diocese of Rochester, New York. He has served on the National Council of Catholic Bishops' (N.C.C.B.) Vocations, and Priestly Formation committees. Currently, he is a member of the N.C.C.B. Administrative Committee, Ad Hoc Committee on Bishops' Life and Ministry, and also chairs the NCCB Committee on Women in Church and Society.

Carroll Cradock is Director of the Child and Adolescent Program at Ravenswood Hospital Community Mental Health Center and a faculty member at the College of Medicine, University of Illinois, Chicago. Dr. Cradock also maintains a private practice in clinical psychology. She has many years of experience in the assessment and treatment of victims of child sexual abuse and in consultation to agencies, parishes, and dioceses regarding community crises resulting from allegations of child sexual abuse.

Jill Gardner is Director of Adult Outpatient and Emergency Services in the Community Mental Health Center of Ravenswood Hospital Medical Center in Chicago. Dr. Gardner, who also maintains a private practice in clinical and consulting psychology, has particular expertise in the area of community level intervention for acute psychological trauma and post-traumatic stress. She has consulted in several parishes and dioceses regarding problems stemming

from allegations of child sexual abuse against church personnel.

L.M. Lothstein earned a doctorate in clinical psychology from Duke University and did post-doctoral work at Harvard University (McLean Hospital). He was for some years associate professor (tenured) at Case Western Reserve University in Cleveland. Dr. Lothstein is currently Director of Psychology at the Institute for Living in Hartford, Connecticut, and associate professor of psychology at the University of Connecticut Health Services Center.

His book, *Female-to-Male Transsexualism,* was published by Routledge & Kegan Paul in 1983.

Patricia A. Moran, ACSW, LICSW, is currently the supervisor of the Sexual Abuse Treatment Team at the Massachusetts Society for the Prevention of Cruelty to Children. She has worked in the field of child welfare for twenty-five years. She received her Master's degree in social work in 1971. Besides clinical work and supervision, she trains professionals on the issues of child sexual abuse.

Father Alan J. Placa is a Roman Catholic priest of the Diocese of Rockville Centre, New York. He has a law degree from Hofstra University and is admitted to the practice of law in New York and in federal courts. Father Placa serves as Vice Chancellor and as Legal Consultant to his diocese, and is a member of the Public Policy Committee of the New York State Catholic Conference. He is a practicing attorney and, in addition to his work in his own diocese, he has served as a consultant to dioceses and religious congregations around the U. S.

Stephen J. Rossetti is a priest of the Diocese of Syracuse, N.Y. He holds M.A. degrees in theology from Catholic University and psychology from Boston College, as well as a Doctorate of Ministry from Catholic University. He was a parish priest for several years before becoming the Director of Education of the House of Affirmation. Author of *I Am Awake,* a Paulist Press best-seller and *Fire on the Earth* recently released by Twenty-Third Publications, Fr. Rossetti is an experienced psychotherapist, spiritual director, workshop leader, and retreatmaster.

Brother Sean D. Sammon, F.M.S., a Marist Brother, is President of the Conference of Major Superiors of Men. Since 1987 he has served as Provincial of the Poughkeepsie Province of Marist Brothers of the Schools. Educated as a clinical psychologist, Brother Sean received his Ph.D. from Fordham University; he lectures widely on issues of concern to religious women and men in the United States and abroad.  His publications include, *Alcoholism's Children: ACoAs in priesthood and religious life* (Alba House) and *Growing Pains in Ministry* (Twenty-Third Publications).

Carol Stanton is Communications Director and member of the bishop's executive committee, Diocese of Orlando, in Florida. She holds a masters degree in religious education from St. Louis University, in Missouri, and has done post-graduate work in radio and television production. She spent ten years in the Orlando television industry as a TV news reporter and anchor with both WFTV, an ABC affiliate, and  WESH-TV, the NBC affiliate. In 1988, she received a Florida Emmy for public affairs programming and has been a Proclaim Awards winner for the past three years for her work in Catholic television programming.

Frank Valcour, M.D. is a graduate of Georgetown University Medical School where he also did his psychiatric training. He is a diplomate of the American Board of Psychiatry and Neurology and a member of the American Psychiatric Association. Other memberships include American Society of Addiction Medicine, National Guild of Catholic Psychiatrists and the International Conference of Consulting and

Residential Centers. He has worked with addicted patients since 1976. He is an associate clinical professor of psychiatry at Georgetown University Medical School.

In 1983 he joined the Saint Luke Institute as Medical Director where he has responsibility for the clinical care provided to both in-patients and out-patients. In his seven years at the Saint Luke Institute he has been involved in the evaluation and treatment of several hundred priests and religious. In addition to his clinical work he has provided educational and consultative services to dioceses, seminaries, and religious communities.